GREAT LIVES OBSERVED

Gerald Emanuel Stearn, *General Editor*

EACH VOLUME IN THE SERIES VIEWS THE CHARACTER AND ACHIEVEMENT OF A GREAT WORLD FIGURE IN THREE PERSPEC-TIVES—THROUGH HIS OWN WORDS, THROUGH THE OPINIONS OF HIS CONTEMPORARIES, AND THROUGH RETROSPECTIVE JUDGMENTS—THUS COMBINING THE INTIMACY OF AUTOBIOG-RAPHY, THE IMMEDIACY OF EYEWITNESS OBSERVATION, AND THE OBJECTIVITY OF MODERN SCHOLARSHIP.

L. JAY OLIVA, *editor of this volume in the Great Lives Observed series, is Professor of History and Vice-Dean, University College of Arts and Science, New York University. He is the author of* Russia in the Era of Peter the Great *and* Misalliance: A Study of French Foreign Policy in Russia During the Seven Years War *and editor of* Russia and the West from Peter to Khrushchev.

GREAT LIVES OBSERVED

PETER THE GREAT

Edited by L. JAY OLIVA

> *Our Peter has neither rivals nor models*
> *since the beginning of the world:*
> *he is akin and equal to no one but himself.*
>
> —VASSARION BELINSKY

A SPECTRUM BOOK

PRENTICE-HALL, INC., ENGLEWOOD CLIFFS, N.J.

To Sidney Borowitz, the best of teachers

C–13–662072–8

P–13–662064–7

Library of Congress Catalog Card Number: 76–126813

Printed in the United States of America

PRENTICE-HALL INTERNATIONAL, INC. (*London*)
PRENTICE-HALL OF AUSTRALIA, PTY. LTD. (*Sydney*)
PRENTICE-HALL OF CANADA, LTD. (*Toronto*)
PRENTICE-HALL OF INDIA PRIVATE LIMITED (*New Delhi*)
PRENTICE-HALL OF JAPAN, INC. (*Tokyo*)

Contents

PART ONE
PETER THE GREAT LOOKS AT THE WORLD

1

The Revolt of the Streltsy, 23   The Social Reforms of 1699, 25   The Defeat at Narva, 26   The Fortification of Saint Petersburg, 27   The Conquest of Narva, 27   The Invasion of Charles XII and the Defection of Mazepa, 29   The Battle of Poltava, 31   Declaration of War Against the Turks and the Founding of the Senate, 38   The Campaign Against the Turks, 40

2

Peter's Preface to the Maritime Regulations, 43   Decree on the Invitation to Foreigners, 44   Three Decrees on the Building of Saint Petersburg, 45   Decree on the Introduction of the New Calendar, 46   Decrees on the Duties of the Senate, 47   Decrees on Compulsory Education of the Russian Nobility, 48   A Decree on Primogeniture, 48   An Instruction to Russian Students Abroad Studying Navigation, 50   A Decree on the Right of Factories to Buy Villages, 51   Table of Ranks, 51   A Decree on the Founding of the Academy, 53   Peter I's Decree Against Peasant Flights, 55   The Peace of Nystadt, 56

Introduction

Peter the Great has been the subject of violent debate and strong opinions in both Russian and world history. Did this stormy but often childlike warrior create the foundations of the new Russia or did he irrevocably destroy the best in Russian civilization? Violent, crude, passionate, eternally in motion, overwhelming in the intensity of his loves and hates, Peter created in his person the impression of great upheaval. The eighteenth century was prone to judge achievements by strength and color of personality, and to the *philosophes* Peter was a magnificent example of the artisan-monarch working tirelessly to enlighten a backward people. Some writers of the early nineteenth century maintained that Russia had no history before Peter and that his great reforms had turned Russia by sheer strength of will from Byzantine backwardness and superstition toward the western road of progress and enlightenment. Others reasoned in arguments closely paralleling those heard in modern emerging nations that Peter, with his western innovations, had forcibly interrupted the logical and natural growth of Russian institutions, thereby corrupting and perverting the native genius of Russian civilization. More recently, Peter the Great has been invoked by those who struggled to justify the work of Joseph Stalin; for them, Peter was a prototype of the lonely reformer working against the misunderstanding and resistance of his people to build the new Russia. For still others, Peter symbolizes the first great era of "modernization," when a strong native tradition came into confrontation with the intellectual and technical stimuli of western Europe; from this perspective Peter is presumed to teach us much about the problems of modern "underdeveloped" nations.

Whatever lessons we may hope to learn from the life of Tsar Peter the Great, two things are reasonably clear. First, the continuity of Russian history was not really interrupted by Peter, but was rather continued and developed; in the strengthening of the autocracy, the imposition of state service on the nobility, the subjugation of the Orthodox church to the state, the cementing of even heavier burdens on the peasantry, the introduction of western technology and administration, the increasing westernization of aristocratic culture, and the expansion of Russia against her northern and southern neighbors, Peter was firmly fixed in the traditions of his fathers. Second, Peter was not a peculiar phenomenon; he must be viewed as one of those aspiring absolute monarchs of the early eighteenth century, who in the pursuit of war and conquest brought about vast changes in the societies over which they ruled. These monarchs, and Peter was one of the chief among them, were the primary builders of the modern world in which we live. Thus, while there are substantial arguments as to what lessons one ought to draw from Peter, there is no argument at all that there are indeed substantial lessons to be learned from his life and work.

Truly the personality of Tsar Peter, even if it did obscure the evolutionary nature of his work, was spectacular by any standards. Son of Tsar Alexis by his second wife, Natalia Narishkin, Peter had nothing in common with his two stepbrothers. Fyodor, a weakling, and Ivan, a mental defective, were both sons of Alexis by his first wife, Catherine Miloslavski. Peter was strong, healthy, and bright from his youth. Born in 1672, he grew rapidly into a giant of a man who stood nearly seven feet tall and weighed over 240 pounds. Peter was a throwback in his line who literally stood head and shoulders above his contemporaries and was a living reproach to his stepbrothers. He had an active and curious mind which delighted in the technical and mechanical but was insensitive to formal education. There was in him all of his life the peculiar quality of a little boy, mixing equal parts of tenderness and devotion with violent strains of cruelty and viciousness.

The death in 1682 of Fyodor II, Peter's half brother, was the signal for open hostilities between the families of Tsar Alexis' two wives, the Miloslavski and the Narishkin. Ivan, the younger brother of Fyodor and the Miloslavski candidate, was clearly incompetent. The Narishkin, under the leadership of Peter's mother, Natalia, proclaimed Peter sole tsar. The boy, then only ten years old, was the tool of his family's ambition. This transient triumph lasted barely a month before undone by the Miloslavski.

Leadership of the Miloslavski had fallen to Sophia, sister of Ivan and Fyodor, who possessed all the spirit and intelligence which her brothers lacked. Her chosen instrument for seizure of power was the *streltsy,* the tsar's bodyguards created by Ivan the Terrible (1555–84) for the city of Moscow. These guards had won special favors over the years, being paid and housed by the state in peace and war. Their duties included the policing of the city and its protection from fires, and service in wartime as the core of the army. In 1682 almost 20,000 of these guards existed in Moscow, a hereditary group with special interests in shops and trade who were jealous of their privileges and of their comfort. It was to this group that Sophia turned for support.

Sophia appealed to the recurrent fears of the *streltsy,* who had been badly abused by the Narishkin in the past. With the help of her lover, Vasili Golitsyn, Sophia worked the *streltsy* into a fury with stories of Narishkin plans for their destruction and rumors that the little Ivan had been murdered. These guards, drunken, violent, and urged on by the clergy, who held that the Narishkin were too sympathetic to foreign influences, stormed into the Kremlin demanding vengeance. Before the eyes of the terrified Peter, the *streltsy* threw Matviev and Ivan Narishkin over the balcony of the Red Stairs onto the waiting pikes below. Some historians date from this childhood experience Peter's reluctance to live or to stay in the city of Moscow which had bred such terror for him.

Sophia emerged victorious from the coup with the title of Regent, and was a forerunner of other determined and talented women soon to come. With Vasili Golitsyn, Sophia dominated the Russian state from 1682 to 1689, but she did not destroy either Peter or his mother in her hour of triumph. Instead the decrepit Ivan V was proclaimed senior tsar, with Peter as junior tsar and Sophia as power behind the throne. The Soviets still exhibit in the Armory of the Kremlin the double throne with the hidden seat from behind which Sophia could whisper instructions to her young figureheads. Real or manufactured, the throne symbolized clearly the situation of these years. There seems little doubt that Sophia desired to be ruler of Russia in her own right, but she never quite dared to seize the crown which symbolized the power she actually exercised. The eight years of her control officially constituted the Reign of Two Tsars, and much of Peter's work was prefigured in them.

While Ivan served as Sophia's ceremonial tsar in the Kremlin, Peter was called to the capital only for special occasions, such as the reception of ambassadors. Most of the time Peter was removed by his mother to the suburban village of Preobrazhenskoe in search of safety and obscurity. This temporary separation from the mainstream of political life explains the relative freedom in which Peter was raised. While his half brother in Moscow was restricted by the traditions and rituals of his office, Peter was freer to roam the countryside and develop his own interests than any Russian ruler had ever been. To the great chagrin of his worried and ever-ambitious mother, Peter eluded his tutors and most education, played constantly in the outdoors, roamed free of guardians, chose his own companions, and soon came into surreptitious contact with the Foreign Quarter.

This relative freedom was combined with a tremendous curiosity. Powerful and intelligent, Peter delighted in mastering all of the technical skills which crossed his path, especially sailing, foundry work, military maneuvers, and later even smithing and dentistry. He was oblivious to ceremony, dress, and honors. A foreign observer remarked accurately that "the Tsar cannot stomach a large dwelling." During his years at Preobrazhenskoe, Peter learned to sail against the wind (a real accomplishment for a Russian), operate a forge, fire artillery, survey, build fortifications, drink like a Prussian trooper, and pursue the ladies. Many of these skills, and especially the latter two, Peter acquired from his early and continuing attachment to the Foreign Quarter.

The Foreign Quarter was the suburb of Moscow where foreign diplomats, merchants, and artisans were required to live in order to avoid contaminating the Russians with their vile western heresies and habits. It was inevitable that Peter should have been attracted by the neat houses, the clean streets, the air of gaiety, the technical marvels, and the sophisticated gentlemen who dwelt there. The Saxon diplomat Franz Lefort became his lifelong friend and tutor, and Peter spent many a night singing, drinking, and smoking in the tavern of the Dutchman Mons. Here he was introduced to skills and marvels which must have stocked his dreams. Here too he found his first mistress, the daughter of the innkeeper.

At Preobrazhenskoe Peter began to exercise his practical nature and growing fund of knowledge in peculiar forms of "play." Around him he accumulated young men of high and low degree to staff his "toy regiments" and to pretend at war. Some of the youths were sent from Moscow to humor the young tsar, while others were recruited by Peter in the streets of the city. Among the last group was Alexander Menshikov, a baker's apprentice who became a drinking companion of the tsar and in later years easily the second most powerful man in the empire. Rounding out Peter's entourage were foreigners like Lefort and General Patrick Gordon, who lent their skills and direction to his "military play." Full-scale battles with real artillery and General Gordon in command rattled the quiet afternoons of Tsaritsa Natalia. In his play Peter prefigured two developments of his reign: the guards regiments, of which the Preobrazhensky and the Semenovsky (a nearby village) were first and most prestigious; and the personal nature of Peter's authority, which extended to men pushed by his will to high place in the state against the privileges of the ancient aristocracy. These latter, the so-called "fledglings" of Peter, were personified by Alexander Menshikov.

By 1689 Peter had still shown no interest in seizing his rightful place in the state. Natalia, attempting to quiet his unbecoming exuberance and limit his night roving, had married him to an attractive but drab and traditional young wife, Eudoxia Lopukhin. Eudoxia contributed nothing to her husband except a son, Alexei, whose fate was to be a domestic and national tragedy. Finding no will in her son to destroy the predominance of Sophia, Natalia finally decided to act for him.

The time was ripe for action. Vasili Golitsyn had returned in 1689 from two disastrous campaigns against the Turks and Tatars in the Crimea. Sophia had hoped to win glory and perhaps the right to rule in her own name by spectacular victories in the steppe, but had made a serious error. The *streltsy* were in an uproar over the necessity of foreign service for protracted periods which ended in nothing but defeat and death. Natalia seized her advantage. Peter was awakened in the dead of the night and told that a plot was afoot at the behest of Sophia to kill him. In dumb terror, Peter was whisked away to the fortress-monastery of Troitsa which had withstood sieges since the Time of Troubles. Some historians maintain that the peculiar twitch which convulsed Peter in moments of great stress dated from this midnight flight. Perhaps no plot existed to kill the seventeen-year-old tsar, but Natalia made excellent use of the rumor.

Natalia issued a call from Troitsa in the name of her son for all patriotic Russians to come to the support of their threatened tsar. Foreign mercenaries like General Gordon, who tested the wind and found it blowing toward Troitsa, heeded the call and made their way to their new leader. Gordon called his defection from Sophia "the decisive break." Slowly the *streltsy* and the merchants abandoned Sophia for Peter. When the patriarch also went over, Sophia knew that her day was done. Vasili Golitsyn was stripped of his lands and exiled, while Sophia was forced to take vows as a nun and enter a convent.

Strangely enough, the year 1689 does not date the real accession of Peter to power. Ivan V, now relegated to the background, continued as co-tsar. The real ruler was Natalia until her death in 1694, while Peter continued to teach himself and his "fledglings" the arts of war. Even after the death of his mother, Peter emerged only slowly into a realization of his powers and his tasks. Two events in the 1690s turned him to those tasks: first, his campaigns against Azov and second, his visit to western Europe.

An example of Peter's place in the general flow of Russian history was his determination to have Azov. In 1695 and again in 1696, Peter followed the river routes to the south, already well-worn by Ivan the Terrible and lately by Vasili Golitsyn, in an attempt to break through the Turks to the warm waters of the Sea of Azov and the Black Sea beyond. Peter went with 60,000 men, himself serving as a lowly apprentice in the rank of bombardier. These campaigns rapidly transformed Peter's military play into military reality, and demonstrated to him the most pressing needs of his military organization: a new core for the army, technical knowledge, supplies, and, the greatest need of all, a navy. The *streltsy* were reluctant, unreliable warriors far from home; Peter found his own guards regiments more loyal and more effective. Peter also discovered that Azov could be provisioned forever by sea as long as the Russians remained landlubbers. Between his first and second campaigns against Azov, Peter, with a Dutch sloop purchased as a model, built the first Russian vessels to sail on the broad Don. Azov was taken and the Russian fleet was born.

The Azov campaigns demonstrated Peter's needs clearly, and these needs in turn produced the "Great Embassy" to Europe. Historians have often debated the reasons for Peter's unprecedented journey abroad in 1697–98; some say that he went primarily to secure an alliance against the Turks; others, led by his American biographer Schuyler, say that he went to become a shipbuilder; still others, Napoleon included, felt that Peter had gone to find spiritual sustenance for his great tasks ahead. To secure help against the Turks and to learn to build ships seem causes enough to suit Peter's personality. In his own words, "a monarch would feel ashamed to lag behind his own subjects in any craft." Peter accompanied this embassy, officially led by his friend Lefort, in the ill-concealed incognito of Cadet Peter Mikhailov. He wished maximum freedom of movement on this momentous journey.

In Europe Peter sought assistance against the Turks in vain; no one was interested. His concern with ships, however, was more easily satisfied. Peter worked as a laboring carpenter in Holland until he believed he had "learned everything a carpenter should know." In England he studied at firsthand the arts of shipbuilding and oversaw the training of his colleagues. An English fellow worker observed that "the Tsar of Muscovy worked with his own hands as hard as any man in the yard." Some Europeans found the tsar a pleasant and charming gentleman; the electress of Brandenberg thought him "a man of great qualities and unlimited intelligence." But most found him a crude and violent barbarian; the duke of Courland spoke for most when he condemned the tsar's excessive drinking, "as if his Tsarist Majesty were another Bacchus." The owner of the house which Peter occupied in England presented an exorbitant bill to the government for the almost complete destruction of the dwelling and gardens which Peter and his rowdy crowd had inflicted. From Europe the tsar sent home all manner of things: foundry equipment, industrialists, technicians, teachers, and instruments to prepare his war machine, and huge slabs of marble, dental equipment, and even a stuffed alligator for his own amusement. The third great naval power, Venice, was on the tsar's itinerary of maritime schooling, but events at home cut short his travels at Vienna.

Peter had left his "fledglings" in Russia, and his accumulating enemies among the *streltsy* had chosen his absence as the best time to strike. Ordered to the frontiers by Peter as punishment for their poor performances at Azov, the *streltsy* rose in revolt in 1698. The revolt proved to be their last. Peter returned with all speed and put down the plot, proceeding to torture and execute thousands of the *streltsy* and to annihilate their organization. Witnesses testified that Peter and Menshikov themselves vied in the chopping off of heads to see who would tire first. Several things of significance were accomplished in the bloodbath. The old and cumbersome military machinery was destroyed in one blow, making way for western army methods and the guards regiments. Further, Peter implicated his unloved wife Eudoxia in the plot, divorced her, and forced her to join Sophia behind convent walls. In doing so, Peter earned the undying hatred of his son.

Upon his return from Europe, Peter was finally ready to assume his tasks. In an age when practically the sole concern of governments was foreign policy, Russia was no exception. Peter took up the threads of a policy long defined by geography and by historical development. He found his work inherent in the Swedish blockade of Russian access to the Baltic Sea, in Turkish use of their client Crim Tatars to block Russian access to the Black Sea, and in the dangerous weakness of Poland lying across the land route to Russia and a prey to Europe's strongest powers. To achieve any major breakthrough which would permit the free flow of goods and ideas from the west to build an enlightened and powerful state, Peter knew that he must make successful war. To insure success in such warfare he had to contrive to make war in the same technical style as his more advanced enemies. The first determination, to war, dominated Peter's reign; and the second determination, to learn how to war against the west in the western manner, generated the whole spectrum of the Petrine "reforms."

Peter's reign was one of constant war. After his failure to secure European aid against the Turks, he made a temporary peace in the south in order to turn against his northern neighbor. Against the Turks Peter could find no allies, but against the Swedes he could find a variety. Northern Europe was overcome by the notion that the new Swedish ruler, sixteen-year-old Charles XII, was weak and foolish, and that his kingdom, bloated by a century of expansion, was now ripe for partition. Russia, Denmark, and Poland opened their war with the supposedly inept Charles of Sweden in 1700. For Peter the prize was the Baltic coast, a spark in the Russian eye since wrested from Muscovy in the sixteenth century. It was the "window to the west" to replace icebound Archangel as the entry for all the technical skills, equipment, and ideas which would refashion Russian power. Peter miscalculated the length of this war. For the next twenty-one years the Great Northern War dragged on, punctuated and later continued by Russian side wars against Turkey and Persia. Peter, intentionally or not, was a full-time warrior and Russia was first and always a war state.

The war began very badly for Russia. The precocious Charles XII drove Denmark from the war almost immediately and turned rapidly eastward to defeat and destroy a Russian army besieging the Swedish fortress of Narva on the Gulf of Finland. Peter himself had been in charge of operations until news of Charles' arrival, when he made a precipitant trip to Moscow to "organize resources." The king of Sweden led his tiny contingent of 8,000 men through a blinding snow-storm in a surprise assault on the Russian besiegers, capturing and killing 8,000 Russians and routing the rest in six hours of fighting. With the victory at Narva achieved, Charles of Sweden made his greatest mistake. Contemptuous of Russian military abilities and sure that he could destroy the Russians almost at will, Charles turned south against the last member of the coalition, Augustus of Poland. Charles left Peter with the commodity he needed most—time, time to organize and to build.

Charles XII spent seven years in the vast flat lands of Poland pursuing the elusive but virtually powerless Polish king. Augustus II, who preferred his native role as elector of Saxony to the elective Polish kingship, was nicknamed "the Strong" more for his size and for the spectacular number of his illegitimate children than for his military prowess. He was finally defeated in 1707. He abandoned his throne to Stanislas Lesczynski, the Swedish candidate, and retired from the war. It was in this period of Swedish preoccupation that Peter organized and trained his forces, undertook an organized campaign to reduce the Swedish posts on the Baltic, dispatched aid to keep Augustus of Poland in the field, and began the erection of the Peter and Paul fortress, later Saint Petersburg, at the mouth of the river Neva. During these years of engrossing toil the tsar, in his own words, "suffered the tortures of hell." The often-told story of Peter appropriating all the church bells in northern Russia after the defeat at Narva in order to melt and recast them as artillery is worth retelling as an example of the tsar's intent to put all resources at the service of his campaign.

By 1708 Charles XII was prepared for the final confrontation with Peter. Victorious in Poland, his reputation rising in Europe as the hero of the day, Charles was now ready for an invasion of Russia. He chose a southeasterly line of march which would carry him into the rich black-soil area of the Ukraine. Charles had decided against a drive on Moscow for a variety of reasons, among them that he could provision his weary troops in the productive Ukraine. He was also reasonably certain of the support of Mazepa, Hetman of the Ukraine, who had long been loyal to Peter but now saw an opportunity to use Sweden to throw off Russian control. Charles sorely needed Mazepa's reinforcements.

As the Swedish march began, the Russians were quick to note the vast length of Charles XII's communications, and a force quickly slipped behind to cut supply lines. After that all went badly for Charles. Mazepa was unable to win general support for his alliance with the Swedes, and Peter, furious at his seeming treachery, established a pro-Russian hetman to split the Ukrainian cause. Then the winter blew down upon the steppe; while Peter's troops were warm and well-fed in winter quarters, the forces of Charles were hungry and ravaged by the cold. Finally, in the thaw of 1709, Peter brought over 50,000 men into the field against the less than 30,000 exhausted troops of Charles XII near the village of Poltava. In his battle orders to his soldiers, Peter vowed that "either Russia will perish or she will be reborn in nobler form." Charles, already wounded in a skirmish, threw his small forces on the entrenched Russians through seven hours of bitter battle. Peter utterly routed the forces of Sweden at the battle of Poltava; more than 3,000 Swedes were killed and 17,000 taken prisoner in the days that followed.

News of the Russian triumph astounded Europe. Charles had built his own reputation in eight years of war and represented a century of unparalleled Swedish power. Charles and Mazepa made their escape south into Turkish territory. Peter wrote to his new wife Catherine: "Little Mother, greetings. I have to tell you that the all-merciful God this day has given us an unequalled victory over our enemies. In brief, the whole of the enemy's army has been clouted on the head and you will hear all about it from us." The most significant battle in eastern European history had ended a century of Swedish dominance in the north, effectively destroyed the independence of the Ukraine, delivered the Baltic coast into Russian hands, and enabled Peter to exercise undreamed power in restoring Augustus as Polish king. Truly a strategic revolution had occurred in northern and eastern Europe, which dawned perhaps too slowly on the great states of Europe. Peter had completed or taken giant steps toward completing the aims of his fathers, and had set the direction of Russian policy for the next two centuries. Henceforth Peter in his letters called Poltava "the Russian resurrection."

Despite Russian victory, the war did not end at Poltava in 1709. Charles XII was far too stubborn and resourceful for that. The Swedish king proceeded to excite Turkish fears of expanding Russian power, and Peter went joyously off to a southern campaign against his old enemies. This Turkish campaign was not successful and resulted in the recession of Azov to the Turks in 1711 in order to escape the war. It was not Peter's destiny to complete his triumph by breaking through to the Black Sea; that was left for Catherine the Great. In the north, Poltava brought Denmark, Poland, and several of the German states back into the war against Sweden. Russia concentrated its attack on Finland, with Peter so confident of ultimate success that he journeyed to Paris in 1717 to seek an alliance, opened campaigns in central Asia, undertook negotiations with China, and later opened a war with Persia over trade routes from the Caspian. The death of Charles XII finally brought the Great Northern War to an anticlimactic end with the Peace of Nystadt in 1721.

From that peace Russia received the territories of Estonia, Livonia, and Ingria, with parts of Karelia and islands in the Gulf of Finland. These lands, the modern areas of Latvia, Lithuania, and Estonia, with parts of southern Finland, gave Russia a long new warm-water coast with a substantial port at Riga and a fortress commanding the Gulf of Finland at Vibourg. In the midst of the triumphant celebrations at Moscow, Peter's Senate voted him the titles of Emperor and "the Great." But even as the emperor's beloved fireworks were fading from the Moscow sky, Peter was back in the north urging on the building of his new city. Saint Petersburg, rising in the midst of the new conquests, was Peter's new capital for his new empire. The city was intended not only to be Russia's European port replacing icebound Archangel, and not only its capital housing the Western techniques which were the keys to Russian power, but also a permanent notice to the Swedes that to retake these territories would require the death of the Russian state. The threat was well understood and Russia went henceforth undisturbed in its new Baltic lands.

The years of warfare demanded a transformation of Russian civil and military institutions and technology in order to make an underdeveloped state capable of meeting and matching its developed neighbors. Machiavelli observed in *The Prince* that the most difficult task for a ruler intent upon war is the "creation of a new order of things." Peter's method for building his new order, once again inherited from his ancestors, was often to borrow and to adapt many of the experiences of his neighbors. The bulk of the "Petrine reforms," then, were the transformations and western adaptations called forth by the needs of a war state.

There was no order, organization, or plan to the reforms in the beginning, although many have since imposed such foresight and planning upon them. The reforms were originally united solely by their contribution to the creation of a war state and by the principle assumed by Peter in propagating them, the concept of state service. Peter held that every citizen high and low owed service to the state, and such services for the war were elicited from every level of society, from the peasantry, townsmen, aristocrats, and clergy. Even Peter considered himself as the first servant of the state. The principle was, once again, not new, but could be traced to Byzantine and Tatar concepts of service, reinforced by the practice of the Muscovite princes. Once again it was not in the originality of his thought but in the energy and extent of its application that Peter's contribution lay.

Obviously the reform of the military reflected the most direct relationship between war and Peter's reorganization. Klyuchevsky recorded a conversation between Prince Jacob Dolguruki and Peter, in which Dolguruki compared Peter with his father and testified that Peter had certainly done well in building the army and extraordinarily well with the navy. Peter replaced the large but temporary and unreliable army units of the past with regular regiments. After the *streltsy* had been struck down, Peter could replace them with aristocrats who were bound to their regiments for life. Especially useful were the elite guards regiments, as the Preobrazhensky and Semenovsky, which were composed of devoted friends and former playmates of the tsar. By 1715 decrees called for one conscript from every seventy-five peasant households, and these were to serve for life. It was a personal disaster for all such conscripted, for army life was miserable and would become worse, but no one could deny that the army thus created was permanent and experienced. Peter's own experience was representative of the new training imposed upon the army which ultimately numbered about 300,000 in a population of 13,000,000. Peter began as a student bombardier and worked his way through every tactic and weapon. The tutors and leaders of Peter's new armies were foreign mercenaries, sometimes of the quality and loyalty of Patrick Gordon and sometimes less reliable.

To Peter alone belongs the title "father of the Russian navy." The first crude sailing ship which he discovered at Preobrazhenskoe and refitted to teach himself is still preserved. Peter single-handedly turned the attention of his cohorts to the sea, fighting a traditional resistance of Russians against the sailor's life. The tsar left behind him nearly 30,000 men in fifty ships of the line, together with innumerable auxiliary craft. This bequest to his posterity, however, was soon to languish. Alexei Tolstoi, in his novel *Peter the First,* noted that Peter was the first Russian tsar to be obsessed by the salt smell of the sea. He was also the last. In any case, in Peter's reign two-thirds of the state budget was allotted to the army and navy.

Decent administration of a burgeoning state structure also required reform. The country was first divided into eight gigantic governments to facilitate taxation and conscription, but later a more workable division of fifty provinces was superimposed. Peter handed over health problems and educational and economic development to the provincial administrations, although little came of it through the century. The Senate was created at the center of government in 1711, an inner group of nine to conduct affairs in the tsar's absence, to act as a high court, and to oversee provincial administrations. The Senate replaced the seniority system of prescribed counselors with the tsar's chosen friends, and was thus an organ of personal power, a contribution to the increased autocracy of the tsar. Finally, in 1718, when Peter was relatively free of the fears of defeat, he began to reorganize old Muscovite offices which were ancient, inefficient, overlapping, and often corrupt. In their place Peter established a then popular form of administration called the "college system." Colleges were administered not by a single minister but by a council of a dozen men who made collective judgments. Colleges were established in areas such as foreign affairs, army, navy, commerce, industry, mines, justice, and finance, and usually included a foreigner somewhere in the second rank to provide experience. The theory was that government by committee provided for the interplay of opinion, but Professor N. Riasanovsky has wisely noted that Peter himself did not have enough decent assistants to place in complete charge of affairs and hoped that administrators in groups would care for one another. The college system lasted until 1803. Finally, in 1722, Peter finished the pyramid of authority by creating a procurator-general over the Senate and colleges to spy out inefficiency and corruption.

According to Louis XIV's finance minister, "money is the sinews of war." No monarch desiring to participate in the revolutionary doctrine of absolutism as practiced by the Sun King could take a first step without financial resources; this truth was infinitely reinforced when the monarch contemplated war. Foreshadowing the problems of Stalinist transformation, Peter could not secure the financial assistance he needed from abroad nor could he obtain it easily or comfortably from his own underdeveloped state. The only answer was to forego easy and comfortable means and to extort money harshly from a Russian population already weighed down by taxes and obligations. Peter established a committee to dream up new impositions, which soon produced innumerable taxes on such varied items as baths, beards, beehives, chimneys, coffins, and clothes. State monopolies on the production and sale of absolutely necessary items, such as salt and vodka, were exploited mercilessly. Finally, Peter ordered the direct tax on land cultivation abandoned, and introduced the head tax (poll tax) for the bulk of the population.

These financial exactions, especially the imposition of the head tax, had far-reaching effects. Aside from increasing the terrible burdens of the peasantry, the new tax necessitated more administrative reforms, such as the census of 1718, to ferret out all available heads. Of the 5.5 million taxable souls, 75 percent were private serfs. One could not now escape the burdens of taxation by simply not tilling land; the peasants were encouraged to farm because they were taxed in any case and would need the money. The head tax, further, lumped together all classes of the peasant population, and in effect made all serfs. The aristocratic power over this great body of enserfed peasantry was increased and enforced in order to hold them to their tasks and insure their availability for taxation and conscription. In a very real way, as the Marxist historian Lyashchenko has charged, the progressive reforms and successful wars of Peter, with their accompanying conscription, labor, and financial demands, were accomplished by enforcing misery and slavery on the mass of the Russian people; Peter was striving to create an "enlightened" state on the backs of an enslaved population. The Russian historian Soloviev records a more straightforward peasant judgment of Peter: "Bloodsucker! He has eaten up the world."

The war also required the development of industry and commerce, and by tradition and by necessity the expansion of the economy could not be left to private hands. Peter, like all great despot-reformers, was in a monumental hurry. "Loss of time is like death," he said, "as hard to return as a life that is ended." He could not afford the luxury of a century of private investment and selection to create an industrial system upon which his great-great-grandsons could depend. "Even if it be good and necessary, yet, if it be novel, our people will do nothing about it unless they have competition." Peter's needs were immediate and so his use of the state as the initiator and often proprietor of enterprises was a natural development. Even where private enterprises were used, they were assisted by guaranteed orders, concessions of serfs, monopolies, and tax exemptions.

In industrial development Peter emphasized a wide range of enterprises. Mining and forges were especially important under the direction of the Demidov family in the Urals, and the production of rough textiles for sailcloth and uniform materials was also emphasized. To staff these varied enterprises, which numbered over 200 by the end of his reign, Peter needed a labor force. But in his empire there was no source of movable labor which could be employed. Consequently, serfs were "ascribed" by Peter from state to land to state and private factories, and Peter issued decrees allowing private serfs to be purchased by entrepreneurs. Thus Peter's industrial interests helped to transform serfdom, the peasant was tied to the land, sold into slavery, a chattel to be bought and sold at will. Once again Peter's advances created new misery for the lower classes.

Finally, Peter turned his attention to Russian commerce. He decreed the transfer of European trade from Archangel to his newly won and newly built Baltic ports at Riga, Reval, and Saint Petersburg. Laws and force had to be employed to bring the conservative Russian merchants to the new ports. Toward that end, Peter ultimately appointed a Westphalian engineer, Münnich, to construct a Volga-Neva canal which was completed after the tsar's death. This, too, was built by enforced peasant labor. Saint Petersburg, thus favored, gained spectacularly in foreign commerce during the first years of its existence. Peter's welcome to the first Dutch ship and the special concessions he promised to others had their effects. In 1710, according to Klyuchevsky, 153 foreign vessels entered Archangel; in 1725, 914 entered Saint Petersburg. Peter left behind him a mercantilist's dream: exports of 2.4 million rubles and imports of 1.6 million. Although most of Peter's industrial achievements, for example a greater production of pig iron than even Sweden, were allowed to languish in the years after his death, the commercial ties with the west which the tsar established continued to grow and strengthen. There was a significant weakness in this development, since Russia developed no merchant marine or carrying companies of its own; trade was firmly in the hands of the English, Dutch, and Hanse cities.

The concept of state service was most organized and defined in the reforms for the aristocracy. Peter's plans for his nobility culminated a long and often bitter struggle in Russian history dating from the days of Ivan the Great (1462–1505), a struggle between ruler and nobility reflected in western national histories of the same period. Peter finally dissolved all distinctions between *pomestie* (an estate which owed service to the state) and *votchina* (an inherited estate which owed no service). Henceforth all nobles were liable to state service at age fourteen and thence until their death, "and they will not receive rank and honor unless they have done so." Peter then established technical schools and academies, and even sent selected persons abroad, in order to provide these state servants with the skills necessary for their work. Peter, lacking any of the alternatives available to his western counterparts, needed the aristocracy to staff his expanding military and civil bureaucracy. The tsar had found a historically based solution to the personnel needs of his war state which took Russia on a slightly different path than that of Peter's western neighbors. In England the aristocracy was exercising power in conjunction with a much-restrained monarch, in Poland the aristocracy shared power with no one, and in France the aristocracy had been replaced in much of the state structure and made ornamental. But in Russia the aristocracy was put forcibly to useful work for the autocrat.

The Russian nobility was enrolled in the new Table of Ranks, or *chin*, whence the Russian word for bureaucrat, *chinovnik*. Place in the table was earned by accomplishment and not by heredity. Finally established in 1722, the table provided civil, army, and navy classifications, with fourteen grades in each. The upper grades were won by outstanding service and/or imperial preference and not by birth, and conferred hereditary aristocracy on the holder; the lower ranks conferred personal nobility only. Exceptions from the table were the elite guards regiments, which were composed completely of selected aristocrats. The aristocratic reform had temporary utility for Peter in staffing his administration, but harbored many dangers which Peter did not foresee. Many of the nobles resisted obligatory service and the removal of their ancient privileges, and the remainder of the eighteenth century witnessed their successful attempts to undo those bonds. Further, the imperial guards at the center of the state promised a century of upheaval in which these nobles would handle the crown of Monomach much as had the praetorian guard of Rome or the Muscovite *streltsy*. Finally, the reform cemented the foundations of the bureaucracy, the formalized body of civil servants who would be so maligned and satirized in the century to come.

Peter's concept of service was extended also to the church. Despite the fact that many of Peter's clerical reforms were firmly in the tradition of Orthodox church subservience to the state following the Byzantine example, some historians have found Peter's most revolutionary change in his actions on the patriarchate. Peter had two motives intertwined in his attitude toward the church: first, he had to have the wealth and lands of the church, a huge percentage of his empire, in order to organize the state for war; second, Peter had encountered heavy clerical opposition to his reforms and to his personal life which he would not long permit. There was first, then, a heavy element of medieval mortmain in Peter's policy: the reluctance to allow the church to set aside lands and wealth as a separate and inviolable preserve in the empire. In the second place, Patriarch Adrian and others condemned Peter's western sympathies, his decrees against Russian dress and the enforced shaving of beards, and his roistering and drunken revels in the streets of Moscow which mocked the ritual and leaders of the church.

When Patriarch Adrian died in 1700, Peter appointed no successor. A Bureau of Monasteries was established to divert church income to state needs. In 1721, when Peter had more time to give to long-range solutions and when the people had become accustomed to an empty patriarchate, Peter issued the Spiritual Regulation. The office of patriarch was abolished; the Holy Synod was established as a government department composed of higher clergy under close government scrutiny. Over the synod was the procurator, a layman appointed by the tsar. A long evolution in church-state relations was finally over; the Orthodox church was now both formally and really a department of the state with duties to uphold the autocracy at all times and in all places. So it was to remain officially until the fall of the monarchy and unofficially far beyond.

Accompanying the formal adaptations of institutions, Peter undertook a campaign to educate at least a small group in the western style. Some historians have held that Peter never looked beyond the borrowing of historical skills from the west, and quote an alleged statement of Peter that "we need Europe for a few decades; later we must turn our backs on it." Still others have seen in Peter's work an attempt to transform the whole of society along "western" lines. It would seem that Peter was interested in more of the west than its techniques, especially in the more relaxed era after Poltava, but he never organized his thought clearly or committed himself completely to the pursuit of such influence. Special schools for the aristocracy were established which were primarily technical, western books were translated in a simplified alphabet which Peter himself had devised, Russian newspapers made their first appearance, the Academy of Sciences was established, Russians were encouraged to dress in western styles and to travel and study abroad, and women were forced out of their traditional seclusion in the *terem*. In order to educate aristocratic ladies and gentlemen in the western manner, the tsar sponsored "assemblies" at which they could practice. Peter himself attended these affairs, insisting that his enforced guests make polite conversation, discuss western topics, and practice western manners. It was Peter also who introduced the western calendar into Russia. In all, Peter only succeeded in applying a veneer of European culture over a small group of his upper classes. In so doing, however, he prepared the way for an ever-widening gap between the Europeanized aristocracy and the unchanging Muscovite lower classes. The Russian historian Karamzin complained a century later that "we began to be citizens of the world but ceased in some measure to be citizens of Russia, and the fault was Peter's."

When the reforms were finished, it was clear that a great many institutional names had been changed and a great many alterations in the structure of institutions had been accomplished, but it was also clear that the essence of Muscovite practice still remained. The emperor was more of an autocrat than he had ever been; the government was one of men and not of laws. Power was still conferred by proximity of person to tsar's favor, and not by title or position. Further, the ideals of the autocrat were still impeded and perverted by the ignorant and stubborn character of his administrators and their corruption. Without the intelligence, honesty, and cooperation of the Russian aristocracy, the reforms could never be more than temporary or semifinished works. Peter himself knew that laxity and corruption "have nowhere in the world been so strong as with us." Peter was indeed a spectacular man, but a man for all that and only one man where thousands were required. The contemporary economic writer, Pososhkov, observed that "the great Monarch works hard and accomplishes nothing; there are few who help him. The tsar pulls uphill along with the strength of ten; but millions pull downhill. How then can his work prevail?" In any treatment which emphasizes the plans and paper projects of the tsar, it is imperative to remember the inertia against which even the mightiest autocracy was forced to struggle and against which it most often fought in vain.

The activities of Peter as they developed and spread were bound to generate opposition on a broad scale. His church reform alienated large numbers of clergy and faithful, while his scandalous orgies, exhibited in the "All-Drunken Synod," only confirmed to the deeply religious that Peter was the Antichrist, sent from the heretic west to pervert and destroy Orthodoxy. Some rumors held that Peter was the illegitimate son of Nikon, the ecclesiastical reformer of his father's reign, or that he was a western agent slipped into the tsar's place at birth. To large numbers of aristocrats, Peter was a tyrant trampling on the prerogatives and traditions of families dating from Rurik the Viking; they saw with bitterness how Peter filled the high offices of state with foreigners and commoners like Menshikov, even to the point of taking as second wife a camp follower of unknown origins, Catherine Skavronsky. And all the while they themselves were bound to civil or military service for life in positions not of their choosing. The Preobrazhensky Office, Peter's secret police, was kept busy ferreting out the resentful and the recalcitrant.

Other resistance was more organized and more violent. The Bashkirs of the southern Urals had risen in revolt against oppressive measures, as had the Tatars and the peasant communities around Astrakhan. Worst of all, in 1707, the Don Cossacks broke into open resistance. Under their hetman, Kondrati Bulavin, the Cossacks were protesting Peter's attempts to extend his taxation and especially his army conscription into their free communities. The Cossacks had long provided refuge for those fleeing Muscovite oppression, and Peter could no longer allow such a "safety valve" to drain the manpower resources of his state. At the very moment he was preparing the face Charles XII and Mazepa at Poltava, Peter was forced to go among the Don Cossacks with 30,000 men and put down their revolt mercilessly and thoroughly. In the same way that Mazepa's defeat with Charles of Sweden ended Ukrainian autonomy, so the defeat of Bulavin extended the sovereignty of the Russian tsar deeper into the southern lands.

There was other resistance, however, much closer to the throne. This was Peter's son, Alexis. The boy, never forgetting that Peter had repudiated and shamed his mother, grew up hating his father and all his works. Married off by Peter to a German princess, Alexis in turn had a son named Peter. Tsar Peter, meanwhile, had chosen a Livonian camp follower who had been in the keep of Menshikov, fallen in love, and married her. This was Catherine, who bore Peter eleven children, only two of whom, Anne and Elizabeth, lived to play a role in Russian history. Catherine and Peter were a wondrously mated couple until their last years, with Catherine alone capable of quieting the storms of temper which more and more overcame the tsar. Alexis, however, found every act of his father and stepmother a reproach. Soon all the aspirations and resentments of clergy and conservative aristocracy were focused on the son. Alexis seemed to promise the end of the reforms and a return to Moscow and its way of life when power was his. When Alexis told his chaplain of his wish to see his father dead, the priest had replied that "God will forgive; we have all desired his death, for the burdens borne by the people are great." Knowing his father's fears and doubts about him, Alexis finally fled abroad. Ultimately induced to return from Europe in 1718, he was charged with treason and tortured to death in the fortress of Peter and Paul, some say with the assistance of Peter himself. The death of the heir had fateful consequences for the eighteenth century.

There were groups who could be called supporters of Peter and his work. First there were the foreigners, the foreign affairs expert Ostermann, General Münnich, and others whose future employ surely depended upon Peter. Then there were the "fledglings" of obscure origins, represented by Catherine and Menshikov, whose high place in the state depended on the will of the tsar alone. Also supporting Peter's work were certain of the great aristocrats won over by privilege or by conviction. Finally, the lesser aristocracy were often sympathetic to Peter's Table of Ranks, his school systems, and his guards regiments, because these provided the poorer, less-prestigious provincial nobility with a road to preferment and honors long denied them. The struggle between opponents and supporters of the reforms was not to be long postponed.

The whole system of the Petrine reforms, their western orientation, their successes and failures, the misery, resentment and resistance which they generated, was embodied in the microcosm of Saint Petersburg. In the words of Andrey Biely in his novel on the city, "Peter and Petersburg, it is all the same." Peter devoted most of his waking hours on the battlefield and off to planning his new capital. Peter wrote to Menshikov from the center of the dismal northern swamps: "I cannot help writing to you from this Paradise; truly here we live in heaven." Situated at the mouth of the Neva as it falls into the Baltic, the city, like Peter's Russia, required superhuman efforts for its creation. The land was marshy and impossible to build upon, so rocks and soil had to be carried miles by hand to provide a foundation. Thousands of peasants conscripted as labor died in the effort among the deadly mists, as in a larger sense they labored and died for all the new works of the empire.

As the aristocracy was bound to service, so were they bound to come and do their service and live their lives in the new city. As Prince Kropotkin noted in his memoirs, to the conservative aristocracy the city came to represent all the new tyranny over their ancient privileges, the western fashions they were forced to adopt, the lives of service to which they were committed. They built their houses and they served, but most hated it. It was no accident that the most impatiently awaited act of Tsarevich Alexis was to return this city to the mud and retrace his steps to the holy city of Moscow. Peter's stepsister Maria voiced a popular curse: "Petersburg will not last after us; let it be a desert."

Peter's command of the state was represented by Saint Petersburg in myriad ways. Insisting, for example, on a stone city and finding no stonemasons willing to come and work, Peter simply decreed that no stonework might be done anywhere in the empire but Saint Petersburg. Very soon the stonemasons came to ply their trade. Saint Petersburg was also symbolic of the new industry and commerce, a window to the riches of the west. The city represented as well the westernization of manners, for here was a specially designed European stage upon which to play out imitations of western culture. The new city symbolized all the affirmations of the new policy: autocracy, westernization, commerce, state service, and conquest. Thus it also represented the same cost as all those affirmations: the misery and enslavement of the people. The city came to symbolize for many aristocrats, most clergy, and all the people, the foreign and forced elements which had come into their lives. Saint Petersburg has remained ever since the city of contrasts.

Peter the Great died in 1725. Characteristically, he had aggravated his condition by wading out in a storm to beach a boatload of sailors about to be swamped. Before his death he had crowned his second wife, Catherine, as his empress, but the succession was in doubt. After the death of Alexis, Peter had assumed the right to name his successor but had not done so. When his last moments came, Peter struggled to scratch the words, "give all to . . . ," but could not finish. The identity of the heir to Peter's power was the dominant and immediate question left by his death.

What, then, did Peter leave behind? He left behind a half-finished structure erected on the foundations of his fathers: an unparalleled autocratic power which culminated a long search of Russian rulers; a territorial expansion to the Baltic which gave Russia its window to the west; a service aristocracy which was already striving to be free of its obligations; a subjugated church which had surrendered its independence to the state for the rest of its existence; the territories of the Ukraine and Don Cossacks bound tightly to the Empire; an industrial development destined to wither and a commercial attachment to Europe destined to grow; a peasantry more tightly enserfed and exploited than it had ever been; the seeds of cultural division between the westernized aristocracy and the backward and uneducated people; and a new capital on the Baltic which symbolized all of Peter's achievements, their cost, and the resistance they generated.

Peter left behind, most importantly for the future, the reputation of Russia as a great power, but without completing the social and economic foundations for sustaining that reputation. In a sense Peter left behind a great deception; Russia had injected itself into the power structure of Europe before it had a well-established administration or a modernized economic and social structure. Peter left to government and reformer alike the task of bringing Russian domestic institutions to the level of Russia's great-power reputation in Europe. It was to be a long and frustrating pursuit.

Finally, Peter left behind the problem of succession. As in Machiavelli's *The Prince,* the problem of personal power which allows of no satisfactory solution is the passing of that power. By what was already a firmly established principle of Russian government and was to remain so for the Soviets, power in the Russian state was passed by no laws or institutions, but by intrigue, violence, and strength. Intrigue and violence at the heart of the state were Peter's last bequests to his successors, both immediate and yet to come.

Chronology of the Life
of Peter the Great

1672	Born; sixth child of Tsar Alexei and first son born of Alexei's second wife, Natalia Narishkin.
1682	Coup d'état by Narishkins and countercoup by Peter's stepsister, Sophia.
1682–89	Regency of Sophia for Peter and his half brother Ivan.
1686	Perpetual Peace with Poland.
1687	Formation of the Preobrazhensky and Semenovsky regiments.
1689	Peter's marriage to Eudoxia Lopukhin and birth of son Alexei; Treaty of Nerchinsk with China; coup d'état against Sophia brings Peter to power.
1695	First campaign against Azov.
1696	Second campaign against Azov.
1697–98	"Great Embassy" to Europe.
1698	Purge of the *streltsy*; Peter's divorce from Eudoxia.
1699	First social decrees on beards and clothes.
1700	Reform of the Russian calendar; suspension of the patriarchate of the Russian Orthodox Church; opening of the Great Northern War with Sweden.
1703	Publication of the first Russian newspaper; founding of Saint Petersburg.
1707	Peter's marriage to Catherine Skavronsky, later Empress Catherine I.
1707–8	Bulavin Revolt.
1708	First major reform of local government.
1709	Battle of Poltava.
1710	Conquest of Livonia and Estonia.
1711	Campaign on the Pruth against the Turks.
1713	Capital moved to Saint Petersburg.
1714	Decrees on entail and noble service.
1718	Decrees on the census and the college system; death of Peter's son, Alexei.
1721	Peace of Nystadt with Sweden.

1722	Issuance of the "Spiritual Regulation"; decree on the Table of Ranks.
1722–23	Campaign in Persia.
1724	Founding of the Academy of Sciences.
1725	Death of Peter the Great.

PART ONE

PETER THE GREAT LOOKS AT THE WORLD

1

The Journal of Peter the Great

Peter the Great ordered a journal to be kept of his affairs beginning in 1698, which he contributed to, edited, and corrected in his own hand up until 1715. It is not possible to determine exactly the various contributions to this journal, since Tsar Peter, as he often did in his writings, refers to himself in the third person. But it is very clear that this journal strongly reflects the tsar's personality, his judgments, and his opinions. Peter was first and foremost a soldier, and the journal reflects his intense interest in the progress of the Great Northern War against Sweden; but at the same time the reader will find intertwined in the narrative clear reflections of the tsar's interests in the reform of his empire. The titles which precede the sections of the journal have been provided to establish the topic and the time.[1]

THE REVOLT OF THE STRELTSY (1698)

It was in 1698, during the journey that His Majesty the Tsar, Sovereign of Russia, made into foreign countries (of which he has fully spoken in his memoir on the war against the Swedes) that four regiments of the *streltsy*, those of Shuvarov, Kalzakov, Hundermarck, and Chernov, which were stationed in the city of Veliki-Louki, revolted and marched against Moscow. His Majesty was informed of this at Vienna, just at the time that he was about to leave for Italy, and these new circumstances obliged him to change his plans. He undertook to return to Russia immediately. After he had passed by Cracow and was a little

---

[1] Peter I, *Journal de Pierre le Grand depuis l'année 1698 jusqu'à la conclusion de la paix de Neustadt*, ed. Prince Michael Shcherbatov (Berlin, 1773), pp. 3–5, 10–11, 30–31, 93, 106–10, 217–19, 228–42, 358–60, 368–72; trans. L. J. Oliva.

distance from that city, he received news that the rebels had been attacked on the road to Moscow and that Boyar and Voivoda Shein with General Gordon had defeated them near the Convent of Voskresensky (the Convent of the Resurrection), which is about forty *versts* from Moscow. The *streltsy* had then been arrested in different places, and the investigation of their rebellion had already begun.

The principal reason for the return of the Emperor into Russia having been removed, he could have then continued his journey into Italy and France. However, he thought that although many of the other *streltsy* had not taken part in this revolt, it would nevertheless be a mistake to place complete faith in their fidelity, since these guards were in the same position as the Turkish *janissaries*. They effectively acted as *janissaries* since they were completely united among themselves, and the suspicions of the Emperor were well founded. This is witnessed by the following: the son of one of the *streltsy*, Steven Moskvitin, thirteen years of age when his father and his uncle suffered the penalty of their rebellion, fled to Astrakhan where he spent four years planning an uprising and finally succeeded in his enterprise, as will be reported below, by inciting a revolt which occurred in Astrakhan in 1705. Thus, Peter feared that a revolution still might take place in his absence, and he persisted in his plan to return into Russia. Passing through Poland, he had a short visit with King Augustus II in the little city of Rawa, where, after having seen some Saxon regiments perform their drills, these two princes were invited by Lieutenant General Flemming to spend the evening with him. Among other proposals that the King of Poland made to the Tsar, he indicated that there were several Poles who were against him and that if they undertook anything against his person, he begged the Tsar to give him his assistance. To which His Imperial Majesty responded that he was ready to do so, but that he did not presume that the Poles would attempt any such action, since in all their history one could never find an example of any such thing. In his turn Peter asked Augustus to avenge the insult which had been given to him at Riga by Governor Dalberg, from which he had hardly escaped with his life. King Augustus promised him he would do so. Thus, after verbally engaging to preserve their mutual friendship, they separated and His Majesty continued his journey towards Moscow.

After he arrived there, trials were carried on for six weeks for the rebellious *streltsy;* some of them endured the final punishment and others were exiled to Siberia. But, far from counting on the fidelity of those who remained, their regiments were broken, permitting each individual to go and establish himself in the village which he thought would suit him best.

Thus, the *streltsy* began to be replaced by truly regular troops, of which eighteen regiments of infantry and two regiments of dragoons were created. They were divided into two divisions; one was under the command of General Golovin, and the other under that of Adam Weyde. The resident of Sweden, Kniperkron, asked the reason, in very strong terms, for the creation of this regular militia, since Russia was at peace with her neighboring states and this was a thing which had never been thought of before.

THE SOCIAL REFORMS OF 1699

In the course of this year we put the printing press on a better footing and began to translate and to print different books dealing with scholarship, artillery, mechanics, and the other arts as well as books of history and some calendars.

A school of marine was opened, and schools for the other arts and sciences began to be introduced gradually. The number of schools for the Latin language was increased, and schools for the German language and for others were founded.

At the same time the Tsar permitted his subjects to leave the country in order to study the sciences in foreign lands. This was forbidden in former times under pain of death, but now not only was permission given for it but many were forced to undertake it.

In this year also the Order of Saint Andrew was instituted, because he was the Apostle of Russia.

His Majesty began also to sign ratifications and letters written to other Christian powers in his own hand. This his predecessors had rarely done, serving themselves with a seal in place of a signature.

The Tsar also judged it appropriate to abandon the ancient Russian costume, which was similar to the Polish costume, in consequence of which he ordered his subjects to dress themselves in the manner of other European peoples and to shave their beards.

When the year 1699 was concluded, he ordered the celebration of the feast of the New Year on January 1st, and the practice of beginning the year on the 1st of September was abolished. He fixed the year 1700 for this celebration in the Cathedral Church of the Assumption at Moscow. The Archbishop Steven of Refan gave a sermon after the mass and a Te Deum was sung on the occasion of the New Year. Three salvos of cannon were fired and there were many fireworks in the place which is called Red Square. Arches of Triumph were also erected in the most remarkable places of the city, and the doors of the palaces of several of the great lords were illuminated and decorated.

The King of Poland after having concluded a treaty against the

Swedes of which we have spoken above, sent his Saxon troops into Courland, and across the frontiers of Livonia, under the command of Lieutenant General Flemming.

THE DEFEAT AT NARVA (1700)

It is incontestable that the Swedes won a magnificent victory over our troops, who were still only an undisciplined militia. In this action we had only one experienced regiment, the one called "Lefortovsky" (which was previously named "Chepelev"), and two regiments of the guards who had participated in the two sieges of Azov and who had never seen action in a prolonged campaign and still less against regular troops. As for the other regiments, with the exception of some colonels, the officers and the soldiers were only recruits as we have shown above. Joined to that was a great scarcity of food, caused by the bad season which prevented us from carrying it with us, so much so that this battle were better called an infants' game than a serious affair. It should not be surprising, therefore, that experienced and regular troops should have had the advantage over troops such as represented us. It is true, however, that this victory caused us great sorrow and made us despair of any happier success for the future. It was even regarded as a mark of the extreme anger of God. But in examining the purposes of Heaven, one sees that they were more favorable to us, because if we had won such a victory over the Swedes at that time, being so little instructed in the arts of war and politics, into what abyss might this happiness have not led us? On the contrary, this prosperity of the Swedes cost them dearly later on at Poltava, although they had so much training and reputation that the French named them the Scourge of the Germans. We, after this terrible setback which was a true blessing in disguise for us, were obliged to redouble our efforts and to make the most extreme attempts to make up by our care and circumspection for our lack of experience. And it was thus that the war was continued, as you will see in the rest of this journal.

After the defeat of Narva the regiments fled in confusion towards the frontiers. The order to rally them and to return them to a good state was given to General Prince Repnin, who arrived in Novgorod with his division and an old regiment called "Boutirskoi," directing his march towards Narva. But he learned on his way of the disaster which had overtaken us and by order of His Majesty he returned to Novgorod.

THE FORTIFICATION OF SAINT PETERSBURG (1704)

His Majesty departed from Moscow and arrived at Saint Petersburg on March 19. He passed by the works at Olonetz, where he examined the buildings that had been begun there.

On May 9, His Majesty went to the Isle of Kotlin, and from there went to Kronslot on a ship called the "Wilkom," or the "Welcome," which had been loaded with artillery which was placed in the new fortification in the presence of the Tsar. Finally, it was decided that the body of troops which had been at the siege of Petersburg in 1703 would attack Karel; and that Marshal Sheremetev, at the head of a body of men who were at the siege of Yanburg and who had passed the winter in winter quarters at Pskov, would go to attack Derpt in Livonia.

THE CONQUEST OF NARVA (1704)

On August 2, two minor officers were captured near Ivangorod; they had been sent to spy out our advanced posts.

On the 3rd and 4th, two soldiers came into our camp, a dragoon and a grenadier, who had defected from Narva.

On the 6th, during divine service, news arrived in our camp that the parapet of the bastion named "Honor" was sliding into the moat, apparently because of the great number of bombs that had been fired at it, and that this material now filled the greater part of the moat. We continued the fire against the bastion and the breach was already considerable. In order to better ruin the flanks, we set up batteries for five mortars near the contrescarpe, from whence they could launch their missiles on the flanks in order to prevent the enemy from defending the breach. A great deal of damage to their cannon was caused by this, in such a manner that on the two double flanks there remained only one cannon of the seventeen that they had had. In the afternoon we sent Colonel Skitte who had been the commander at Derpt and who was now a prisoner, to speak with General Horn, commandant of Narva, and to assure him that the city of Derpt had been taken, and instructing him at the same time how His Majesty had acted toward those over whom he had been the commander and toward his garrison. Marshal Ogilvy also sent to the Commander of Narva a messenger with a letter in which he informed them of the taking of Derpt. But Horn did not wish to receive it, and some officers spoke for him. However, he promised to respond the next day to the letter, asking at the same time to suspend hostilities until then. But the Marshal did not wish to consent to this, and sent him the same evening a letter from Colonel Poviche in which he begged him to surrender the place, representing to him that the breach was already made and that God himself had overthrown the bastion "Honor." He promised him in addition, in the example of other garrisons, the good graces of His Majesty, and offered him an honorable surrender, adding that if, on the contrary, he did not wish to surrender and we were obliged to make an assault, then there would be no more propositions and neither grace nor surrender would be available. This letter told the Commander that by the following morning he should make a response in writing by a messenger. During this time, our cannonade and bombardment continued unabated, in order not to give the enemy time to repair his fortifications and the breach in the walls. We also made a line on the contrescarpe for our musketeers so that they could support the troops who were going to have to make an assault.

On the 7th, the Commander of Narva sent a messenger with a written response in which he said that he could not surrender his command without an order from his King, but that he hoped to defend it until the King came to his aid and that he would await this last extremity. He added at the same time certain insulting expressions. On the same day, a General Council of War was held in which it was decided to make a general assault on Narva. Marshal Ogilvy gave the orders to distribute orders to all regimental commanders to this effect.

On August 8th, the scaling ladders were secretly carried to the approaches and the grenadiers of all the regiments were prepared; infantry as well as cavalry. They were ordered to throw grenades continually, in support of the portable mortars which were placed on the bastions. In addition, across from the bastion named "Victoria," on the contrescarpe, we established a battery of four cannons in order to cover the assault.

On the 8th, during the night, the people involved in the assault were sent into the trenches, others were prepared to cover the assault, and still others were arranged to support them. On the morning of the 9th, the rest of the infantry left the camp and arranged themselves near the approaches. Soldiers who were under punishment were ordered to carry the ladders into the moat; these soldiers were those who had deserted and they were ordered to place the ladders against the smashed bastion called "Honor." On the same day at two o'clock, the assault was launched, following a signal given by five mortars whose bombs were thrown against the bastion "Victoria." Here a breach was made under the command of Lieutenant General Schembeck. Major General Chambers attacked the bastion "Honor," whose front was destroyed. Major General Scharf's command attacked the barriers which protected the bastion "Gloria." Since the ladders were mounted everywhere, the fortress was weakened on all sides; the officers and the soldiers advanced with so much valor that, without regard to the strong resistance of the enemy nor to a mine that had been exploded in the breach, nor to the great number of explosions that rolled during three-quarters of an hour, our men mounted the bastions, first on "Honor" which the soldiers of the Preobrazhensky and other regiments assaulted under the command of General Major Chambers. By their fire they obliged the enemy to abandon the walls. Finally, attacking the breach and crossing the ditch of the third bastion, they pursued the enemy into the old stone city.

The Commander, seeing so vigorous an attack, ordered the gates of this ancient city closed without delay and had his drummers beat the alarm; he himself took a caisson on which he beat with his dagger. But our troops ignored all this, killed several drummers, mounted the walls and forced the gates. Then, pursuing their advantage with the same strength, they entered into the castle and massacred a large number of the Swedes. The Commander of Ivangorod hardly had time to close the door of the gates of the city, because they were filled with the enemy fleeing through the gates and spilling over all the outside works. The engagement lasted less than two hours. Thus, the prideful Commander of Narva, by his pig-headedness, caused the loss and the ruin of the garrison and of its citizens. And if we had not held back the fury of the carnage, few would have escaped. On the same day a private secretary, Pierre Schapirov, was sent to Ivangorod in order to tell the commander to surrender without delay and to put himself at the mercy of His Majesty, and that, in the case that he did not, no mercy would follow. To which an officer responded in the Commander's name, that one ought to accord him time in order to hold council and to send his reply in writing.

This victory of August 15th was celebrated at Narva with ceremonies of thanks to God, accompanied by the firing of artillery and of muskets.

On the 16th, the Commander of Ivangorod, after some negotiations, surrendered. He was allowed to exit from the garrison with his troops under arms but without flags or drums. And following their request they were escorted a part of the way by the land and a part of the way by the sea, as far as Reval and some even as far as Vibourg.

THE INVASION OF CHARLES XII AND
THE DEFECTION OF MAZEPA (1708)

On that same day the enemy soldiers who were in the little village of Schepleevka placed their cannons on the mountain where their camp had been arranged in three ranks, with the first at the summit, the second in the middle, and the third at the foot of the mountain.

They began to fire on our troops. Although our troops were protected by a parapet, the land was so flat that a rank of men could hardly be covered by the parapet and it was impossible to put them in four ranks because of the enemy fire. This obliged us to quit the position and to retire to Voronets. The enemy then was able to cross the Desna.

On the 3rd, we arrived at Voronets where we spent some time; and there we received news from Prince Menshikov who told us that he had seized, without great loss of men, the city of Baturin where the traitor Mazepa made his residence. Menshikov had also captured the principal criminals, Colonel Schetchel and General Kenigsek, with some of their adherents. The rest were massacred and the city burned and levelled to its foundations. They found there also Mazepa's treasure. There was also a great arsenal prepared for the Swedes by Mazepa, and this was burned.

In consequence of this news, the troops went to Gluchov, where His Majesty arrived on the 5th.

General Prince Menshikov came there from Baturin the next day.

On the 7th, by order of His Majesty, the Cossacks, following their custom, chose by a voice vote and by plurality the Colonel of Staradoup named Ivan Skoropadski as their new Hetman.

On the 8th, the Archbishops of Kiev, of Chernigov, and of Periaslavl came to Gluchov.

On the 9th, these Archbishops decreed a solemn excommunication against Mazepa, and the same day the portrait of this traitor, with the cord by which it had been suspended removed, was put into the hands of the executioner who attached a rope to it and dragged it through the streets and public places up to the gallows where it was hung.

On the 10th, Colonel Schetchel was executed at Gluchov with the other traitors and followers of Mazepa who had been captured at Baturin.

On the 16th, His Majesty left with his troops and spent the night at Krasnaya, from which he departed on the 19th and arrived the same day at Terni.

On November 20, having left Terni, His Majesty arrived the same day at Horugevka, where Prince Menshikov apprised His Majesty of the fact that some Circassian peasants along the Desna had massacred and made prisoner nearly 150 Swedes.

On the 21st, His Majesty arrived at Olchanka and on the 22nd moved to the little village of Markovka where he remained until the 24th. He then began a march for Tutivl in the midst of a great cold and frost. The troops traversed a desert and finally arrived at a town called Michalovka. It was then that it was resolved to put a garrison at Poltava and to send Colonel Kelim there with five battalions.

On the 26th of November, His Majesty arrived with his troops at Lebedin.

We then had news that the King of Sweden was marching toward Romna.

On the 30th, His Majesty was in a little city of Veprik, where we had a strong garrison of 1,500 men. And in its suburbs, in the villages, there were regiments of dragoons under the command of Lieutenant General Renn. From here His Majesty went to reconnoiter Gadiatch where there were three regiments of the enemy. On December 3rd, His Majesty returned to Lebedin.

Finally, one held a council of war where it was decided that the greater part of the troops would move on Gadiatch, and that General Allart would march toward Romna where the general quarters of the King of Sweden were located. There was purpose in these movements: in case the King did not go to the aid of Gadiatch, General Allart would not approach Romna and we could continue the siege of Gadiatch. But in case the King of Sweden did go to relieve the town, General Allart would enter Romna and we would then lift the siege of Gadiatch. We would then be able to make one or the other of these two moves, whichever might be appropriate.

THE BATTLE OF POLTAVA (1709)

On the 13th of May, General Prince Menshikov reported that the enemy was besieging the city of Poltava, and that already the enemy had made several violent assaults on the town but that they had been repulsed with considerable loss. He reported that our troops with their sorties had killed many of the enemy. However, this city was still strongly blockaded. Consequently, we resolved, following the advice of all our generals, to make a diversion. On the 7th of May, we detached a great corps of our troops, cavalry and infantry, and sent a part under General-Major Belling along the course of the river Vorskla in order to approach Opotchna from the rear, and the other part under General Menshikov to attack the enemy directly against his trenches on the other side of the Vorskla. In order to achieve these plans, it was ordered that three bridges be built that same night, and it was agreed that when the troops would have passed these bridges General-Major Belling would begin the attack on the enemy at Opotchna. The rest of the troops commanded by General Prince Repnin would hold themselves ready to give aid to whichever of the two detachments would be most exposed. As soon as the first, under the command of General Prince Menshikov, had passed the river, then, on the morning of the 7th, the infantry crossed the bridges and the cavalry swam the river.

The crossing was made without regard to the terrible cannonade which the enemy launched from his fortifications nor to the difficulty of the passage. Having surmounted these obstacles, our soldiers advanced toward the enemy fortifications sword in hand, storming them with a great loss and obliging the enemy troops to disperse. These fortifications contained four squadrons of cavalry and 300 infantry. Our troops pursued the enemy as far as Opotchna and three regiments of Swedish cavalry and two regiments of infantry had come from Opotchna to aid them and inserted themselves into the order of battle. However, at the first encounter the Swedes fell into chaos and retreated toward Opotchna, setting fire to the suburbs and locking themselves in the castle. Then our troops, having learned that the King of Sweden was coming himself at the head of seven regiments and that General-Major Belling could not arrive in time because of a difficult passage and the long detour that he was obliged to make, disengaged from the enemy and retired in good order. In this fight, 600 of the enemy died on the field and we took from them two cannons with their munitions, two flags and two drums.

Prisoners: major—1, captains—3, lieutenant—1, ensign—1, lower officers and soldiers—300.

At the same time we freed a certain number of Ukrainians, whom the enemy had taken in different places and was using to work on different fortifications.

About 600 of our dragoons and grenadiers were killed or wounded.

Finally, our whole army advanced to the edge of the river Vorskla, and established itself directly in front of Poltava, across the river and in view of the enemy's camp.

At the same time, Brigadier Alexei Golovin was sent with 900 men to fortify the garrison at Poltava. He happily entered into the city in full view of the enemy.

On the 15th, we sent a party of light cavalry to the other side of the Vorskla, where it raised the horses which the enemy had collected, and, having killed the guards, stole about one thousand horses. At the same time we captured some servants of Major General Krous.

On May 17th, we detached a corp of about one hundred grenadiers and posted them by the bridge across the Vorskla on which the enemy had established a well fortified redoubt. Others attacked the enemy with great courage and routed them in a difficult fight. But because of the deep marshes which our troops were obliged to cross by wading up to their chests while pursuing the enemy, and without time to regroup, the enemy was able to stop and begin to pour a furious fire of musketry and cannon on our troops. As a result we lost about twenty grenadiers and were obliged to retreat.

During this time our garrison at Poltava made a sortie and attacked the enemy posts at the base of the mountain with so much courage that they were routed from their advance positions and fled towards the river's edge. However, as the enemy continually sent additional aid to their posts, our men retreated in an orderly manner into the city without being pursued. This sortie lasted about a half-hour. Several hundred Swedes perished and still more were wounded. Our cannon opened fire on the enemy from our fortifications and were so successful that they forced the Swedes to quit their advance posts. We continued to work on our fortifications during the day in full view of the enemy and established a strong redoubt a few feet from the bridge from which we fired with great effect. We worked even during the night without being disturbed or impeded by the enemy, and continued on the 18th and into the following night. On the night of the 18th, our Valaques crossed the Vorskla and killed those who were guarding the horses and removed about two thousand which they brought to our troops.

On the 19th of May, we received news of the destruction of the fortress of the Zaporogian [Cossacks], called the Sech, in which these Cossack traitors had barricaded themselves. We had sent Colonel Peter Jakovlev with a party of cavalry to perform this task, and he took the place, killed many of the Zaporogians, and razed this haven of thieves.

Up to the 27th of May, His Majesty was at Troitzk handling several general matters related to the army and navy. These matters had been accumulating because His Majesty had not been able to occupy himself with problems of the navy for almost ten years.

His Majesty left Troitzk on the 27th to join the army which was drawn up near Poltava.

On the 31st, His Majesty received news from Field Marshal Goltz, who was in Poland with some auxiliary troops, that he had sent a party of 1,500 dragoons against the Polish troops at Ledukov under the command of the Starost of Bobruisk, Sapiha, who commanded 5,000 regular troops not counting the Polish militia. Our men had won a great victory because they fell upon the enemy without warning and totally defeated them. Several prisoners were taken and several were killed. Those killed amounted to forty-eight men.

His Majesty joined his army at Poltava on the 4th of June, and on the 13th he wished to cross the Vorskla with his troops and to march against the enemy. But because of the difficulties of the river crossing, he was not able to execute this maneuver and returned to the former posts.

During this time, our Lieutenant Colonel Jarlov sent a letter by a spy in which he told us that he was among our prisoners captured at Veprik, and now kept at Staroi-Senschar, but that only a few of the enemy were guarding them. As a result, we sent a party of dragoons commanded by Lieutenant General Heinchin, who informed us on the 14th of June that he had taken the city, that several hundred Swedes had been killed, and that he had freed about 1,000 of our men. Among them was Lieutenant Colonel Jarlov, who, when he heard that our troops were attacking the enemy, killed his guards and joined our troops.

On the 15th of June, Lieutenant General Renn took some regiments of dragoons and irregular cavalry and crossed the Vorskla near the enemy camp. He posted two regiments of dragoons in an ambush in the woods. Following that he sent a party of 500 dragoons and all of his irregular cavalry to the Swedish camp in order to draw them out. This stratagem succeeded because, when the Swedes saw this advance party, the King himself at the head of six regiments came out to meet them. And as our troops fled toward the woods where our other dragoons had been stationed, the enemy furiously pursued them. They were then received by violent fire from our hidden troops and were obliged to retreat. Our troops pursued them in their turn across a great plain where they killed several Swedish soldiers. Finally, the Lieutenant General, without having suffered any loss at all, recrossed the Vorskla but left his troops on the other side in order to maintain free passage of the river.

At this time we held a council of war in order to decide on the manner of liberating Poltava without giving a general battle, which we regarded as a very hazardous thing. It was decided then that we would confine ourselves to building fortified approaches to the city.

On the 16th of June, these new approaches were begun to provide communication with the city; but the Swedes impeded our work with their transverse line, and the river and the marshes also placed obstacles in our way. During this time, we communicated with the city by sending in letters in empty bombs fired over the enemy lines. They did the same thing from inside the city, and reported to us that powder was running out and that the enemy had approached the palisades and begun to sap the ramparts. Although our troops had constructed a trench, they could not remain there for long. Therefore, a great council was assembled at which it was resolved that we should cross the river and engage in a general battle as the only means to save the city.

On June 19th, our army began to cross the river two miles above Poltava, where General Renn had established himself with his cavalry.

On the 20th, our whole army had passed the Vorskla, camped on the other side, and prepared its fortifications. Finally, on the 25th, the whole army began to advance and stopped that evening about a quarter of a mile from the enemy. We were organized so that the enemy could neither oblige us to participate in a general battle before we had made our fortifications nor surprise us. The trenches were built in a single night. Our cavalry was on the right in the woods, having before them redoubts provided with men and cannon. Brigadier Aigustov had command of them.

On June 25th, it was learned that the King of Sweden was advancing in person to survey the Russian camp; that night he encountered a party of Cossacks seated around a fire who were not on their guard and he and his group had approached them, had gotten off their horses, and the King himself had killed one of the Cossacks with a rifle shot. The Cossacks jumped up, fired three shots at him, and wounded him in the leg, a wound which caused him a great deal of pain.

On the 26th, His Tsarist Majesty himself examined the place as well as the enemy camp in order to plan with most possibility of success. But the enemy, with his boldness and his usual pride, beat us to this, and we are going to tell the story of the manner in which they undertook the action.

On the 27th, in the morning but still in the shadows of night, the enemy fell upon our cavalry with his cavalry and infantry. The attack was made with such fury that it seemed sufficient to destroy our cavalry and to overrun our redoubts. However, there was a great deal of resistance and the enemy could take only two redoubts that we had begun the same night and which were still not finished. As for the others, they were not taken; on the contrary, six battalions of enemy infantry and a dozen squadrons from their right wing were separated from the rest of the army and obliged to flee into the woods. The principal body of the enemy army passed between our redoubts and suffered severe losses; fourteen standards and flags were seized by our cavalry, who several times obliged the enemy cavalry to separate. But the enemy cavalry was constantly receiving assistance from its infantry, and our own infantry could not sortie from its fortifications in order to assist our cavalry (to which we must add that Lieutenant General Renn was badly wounded in this furious struggle). Therefore, Lieutenant General Baur was ordered to retreat on the right flank to the fortifications in order to permit the infantry to come forth. However, it was recommended to him to keep the mountain on his flank and not behind him, so that the enemy would not be able to pin our cavalry to the base of the mountain. Further, he was ordered to retreat only in case he was attacked by enemy infantry; if he was attacked only by cavalry he ought to hold firm and beat them back. These orders were followed exactly, and, when General Baur began to retreat, the enemy who advanced against him had our fortifications on their flank from a left angle; General Levenhaupt with his infantry approached to a distance of thirty paces and was then repulsed by our cannons. Finally, the enemy saw that he could gain nothing by pursuing our cavalry and retreated to restore order again outside of cannon range in a plain which was in the middle of the woods. At the same time General of Cavalry Prince Menshikov and Lieutenant General Renzel were sent with five regiments of cavalry and five battalions of infantry against the cavalry and infantry that had been separated from the enemy army and who had hidden in the woods. These generals charged the enemy and by the grace of God totally defeated them and made prisoner General Major Schlippenbach. Major General Rosen retreated towards his lines at the foot of the mountain and took refuge in his redoubts. Lieutenant General Renzel followed him and surrounded him; he sent a messenger to demand his surrender but the enemy asked for time. They were accorded only a half-hour, at the end of which Major General Rosen and his troops emerged from their redoubts, laid down their arms and surrendered. At the same time our infantry sallied forth from both sides of the fortifications, so that in case of an enemy counterattack we would be able to draw freely on them from these fortifications. But when we saw that the enemy was still in disorder from his attack between our redoubts, and that he was attempting to restore order among his troops in the middle of the woods, then we also sent out the infantry which was lodged along the front of our fortifications. Having at this point taken six regiments of cavalry from our right wing, we sent them behind the infantry on the left wing. It was thus that our army ranged itself in order of battle and resolved to attack the enemy.

Finally, with the aid of God, we charged against the main body of the enemy army, which, without waiting our attack, advanced on us. Thus, at nine o'clock in the morning the action began between our left wing and right wing of the enemy; a little later the front lines of the two armies engaged in the combat, and although each side furiously beat against the other and exchanged the most vicious fire, all this lasted only two hours. The invincible Swedes, cavalry as well as infantry, were overwhelmed with little loss on our side. The Swedish troops did not once stand in place, but attacked without interruption. We assaulted them with sword and with bayonet, and slowly pushed them back to the woods where they had prepared themselves before the battle. On this occasion Major General Stackelberg was made prisoner as well as Major General Hamilton, Marshal Reinschild, the Prince of Wurtemberg, several Colonels and other officers, as well as the subalterns and some thousands of soldiers of whom the majority were taken with their arms and their horses. On the field of battle and near the redoubts were the bodies of 9,234 enemy soldiers, not counting the bodies dispersed in the woods and the fields and those who were dying of their wounds of which we were not able to count the number. The King of Sweden, being wounded, was carried in a litter during the battle. This litter was made of pikes and one side of it was struck down by a cannon shot. As to the cannons, the flags, and the drums that we took, there is attached here a list as well as a list of those of our troops who were killed or wounded in this action. Thus, by the grace of the all-powerful God, this victory, to which there has been nothing similar in our history, was won with little pain and little bloodshed over the prideful King of Sweden, by the prudent and courageous conduct of His Majesty the Tsar in person and by the valor of his generals and soldiers. In this momentous affair His Majesty exposed himself for his subjects and for the country without care for his person, as a true and great captain. His hat was pierced with bullets and a bullet was found in the wooden part of his saddle. Let us add that in this combat it was only our first line of forces which took part; the second line of our army did not have time to join the fight.

After this happy event, His Majesty dined in his camp under his tent with all his generals, officers, majors, and subalterns, as well as with some Swedish generals who had been taken prisoner in the battle. Count Piper, a Swedish minister, seeing that he could not save himself, came of his own accord to surrender himself at Poltava, with the secretaries of the King of Sweden, Cederhelm and Diben. At Poltava he was taken to the tent of His Majesty and dined at the same table with him and found there also the Swedish Marshal Reinschild and other generals. His Majesty praised the courage and the valor of Marshal Reinschild, offered him his own sword and permitted him to carry it. The same day, in the evening, the army was ordered to pursue the rest of the enemy; this enterprise was under the command of Lieutenant General and Colonel of the Guards, Prince Golitsin, at the head of the guards regiments, and Lieutenant General Baur at the head of the regiment of dragoons. The next day, that is to say the 28th of June, Prince Menshikov was sent also.

On the 28th, the Swedish Major General Meyerfeld came to Poltava, under pretext of some commission on the part of the King of Sweden. It was decided to detain him and to include him among the other prisoners, because not only did he have no letters of credence but he did not even have a passport. Finally, he gave his parole and begged to be allowed to leave for Stockholm and he was placed under the guard of Major General Buturlin.

On the 29th, the name day of His Majesty, ceremonies of thanks to God took place on the battlefield for this famous victory, and this act of devotion was accompanied by three salvos of artillery.

On the 30th, His Majesty put the army into motion in order to follow the enemy. But although we pursued them with great diligence, as they had abandoned most of their equipment and were making rapidly for the Dnieper, we could only reach them by the 30th of June when we encountered them drawn up at the foot of a mountain near Berevolotchna on the edge of the Dnieper. Here we learned from a quartermaster of a regiment and from some soldiers who had been captured that only three hours earlier the King of Sweden with a few hundred guards had crossed the Dnieper with a great deal of difficulty. With him also were Major Generals Sparr and Lagerkron. He left the command of the rest of the army to General Levenhaupt. General Prince Menshikov, without losing any time, approached Berevolotchna with his unit which was not more than 900 men. But, as we learned from the prisoners that we had taken, the enemy was not really interested in giving battle. Menshikov asked Levenhaupt to surrender, assuring him that all possibilities of retreat and hope of salvation were vain and that it was only reasonable to do so. Menshikov warned him that if he did not surrender he could not hope for any quarter. Thereafter, General Levenhaupt sent Major General Kreitz to General Prince Menshikov along with Colonel Duker, Lieutenant Colonel Trautseter, and the aide of the General, Count Dougles. After some conversations, General Prince Menshikov and General Count Levenhaupt concluded and signed a surrender, following which the enemy, about 14,000 men of whom the majority were cavalry, stacked their arms and became prisoners of war. Lieutenant General Baur took charge and received all of their artillery, their military equipment, their flags, standards, drums, and trumpets. Thus, by the grace of God, the whole of this famous enemy army which during its campaign in Saxony had become the terror of Europe, fell into the hands of His Tsarist Majesty. No one escaped; everyone surrendered to the victorious arms of Russia except a few hundred men who had crossed the Dnieper with the King of Sweden and had fled into the states of the Turk. Even of those, 200 had been killed and more than 260 had been made prisoners by a party of our troops. . . .

DECLARATION OF WAR AGAINST THE TURKS AND THE FOUNDING OF THE SENATE (1711)

February 25th, a feast day, His Majesty participated in a Te Deum, which was sung in the Cathedral Church of the Assumption, and published there a manifesto on the breaking of the peace by the Turks, begging God to give His aid against the breakers of the peace and the enemy of the Christian name.

Two regiments of the guards paraded before the church, and in place of their usual white flags they carried newly made red flags with the inscription: "For the name of Jesus Christ and for Christianity." And higher up surrounded with a shining cross one could read the device: "In this sign conquer." These regiments marched the same day for Poland in order to join the great army of Count Marshal Sheremetev.

On the 2nd of March, in the same Cathedral Church of the Assumption, in the presence of His Tsarist Majesty, the new Senate and the governors took the oath of office to fulfill their charges with honor, integrity, and energy, to be faithful to their Sovereign and to the state and to be just in the affairs of individuals as well as in the affairs of the state, and to act always in good faith in the raising of money and men and in other things relative to the interests of His Majesty and the state.

After that, on the same day, His Majesty sent instructions to the new Senate charging them to evaluate and punish iniquitous judges by removing their honors and their property, a punishment which was intended to end judgments made in bad faith. He also enjoined the Senate to investigate waste across the whole extent of the empire and all the expenses which were not necessary, and above all, those which were the subject of corruption.

Also, noting that many commoners had become army officers and that the nobles avoided service and hid themselves in their villages, His Majesty sent an order to the Senate to assemble all the young nobles and to take down their names for military service, above all those who were avoiding such service.

His Majesty ordered also the establishment in all of his states of *fiscals* and ordered that a *fiscal-general* be put at their head, in order to spy out and take public information related to injustices and all things prejudicial to the state, and to inform the Senate of all of these.

He ordered also the conscription of an army corps to replace the one which had been stationed in Livonia and which had suffered great losses. These recruits were to be from the frontiers of Wallachia, toward which Marshal Count Sheremetev was now marching.

At the same time General-Admiral Count Apraxin was ordered to go to Azov, in order to examine the state of those territories and to defend them against the Turks. With regard to the Cossacks of the Don and to the Kalmuks, they were to be brought into action in the springtime against the Turks and the Tartars by land and sea, pursuing them as the occasion might demand. Major General Buturlin and the Hetman of the Cossacks Skoropadski received orders to lead eight regiments toward Kamennoi-Zaton, there to observe the movements of the Turks and Tartars; if these enemies advanced, they were to defend against them to the last extremity.

On March 6, it was solemnly announced that Her Majesty the Tsarina Catherine Alexievna was the true and legitimate wife of the Emperor Peter I.

The same day, after having made all the arrangements of which we have spoken at Moscow, His Majesty, accompanied by his wife, left to join the army which was in Poland. Their Majesties were joined by ministers and other court officers; they journeyed through Viazma, Smolensk, Gorki, and arrived at Slutsk on the 13th, where they found the infantry regiments of Count Sheremetev. Their Majesties remained there until the 18th because the roads were still nearly impassable. . . .

THE CAMPAIGN AGAINST THE TURKS (1711)

An envoy of the Hospodar Constantin Brankovan of Multianck, after paying his respects to His Majesty, told him that the Grand Vizier [of the Turks] had ordered the Patriarch of Jerusalem to discover through the intermediary of the Hospodar whether His Majesty had any dispositions to peace which he would receive by order of the Sultan. But we placed no confidence in this message and did not wish to hear any proposals, for fear of inspiring the enemy with too much confidence.

A council of war was then held to plan the campaign, and occupied itself primarily with the problem of provisions; practically nothing would be found to support us in such a ruined country as Wallachia [part of modern Rumania]. It was decided to gather our troops near Jassy and to build up our supplies there. However, it was learned that the Turks had still not completely moved their troops over the Danube; the Hospodar and the nobles of Wallachia begged His Majesty to intercept the Turks on the Danube, telling him that there were large stores of supplies amassed by the Turks in Multianck, in the villages around Brailov, which were undefended. This was confirmed by the Envoy of the Hospodar of Multianck and by Count Thomas Cantacuzene. Although it was dangerous to follow their advice, His Majesty did not want to throw the Christians who sought his aid into despair and consented to this perilous enterprise to secure supplies. After many meetings it was agreed to try to meet the enemy on the Danube. It was resolved to march our troops along the right bank of the River Pruth so that the river would be between us and the Turks up to the town of Faltzi; the enemy could not cross the river because of the large swamps above the place. From there General Renn could take half of the cavalry by way of the woods to the River Ciret to seize the provisions mentioned above; afterward, Renn could rejoin the regular army at Galatia, form a supply station, and seek out the enemy.

This plan worked up to July 7. On the evening of that day we received unexpected news from General Janus, whose cavalry was preceding our infantry by two miles. He reported that the enemy had already crossed the Pruth, and we ordered him to pull back to our main force. It was later revealed that this report was false, because the Turks had not crossed the river and were still on the other side, and Janus could have stopped them if he had been a man of honor. However, he retreated and thereby encouraged the Turks, who then crossed the Pruth and followed him with their light troops and their elite cavalry. But when His Majesty himself went to meet General Janus with an infantry party, the Turks dispersed and enabled Janus to rejoin the army without casualties. Thus the enemy prevented us from carrying out our plans to besiege Faltzi and crossed the Pruth with their whole army. This cut communications between our army and that of General Renn, so that His Majesty decided to detour his march towards Ciret; but the high mountains and scarcity of water cancelled this plan. Further, all the army horses were seriously weakened by lack of forage, since the frosts had killed the field grasses to the root. The divisions of Generals Veid and Repnin were still behind, and a war council, held to discuss this unforeseen problem, resolved to retreat so that the whole army would be reunited and then to give battle to the enemy. In the evening the army began its march, and linked up with the divisions of Veid and Repnin that same night.

On the 9th, in the morning, the Turks attacked our rear guard with their cavalry and infantry. Only the Preobrazhensky Regiment was in the rear guard, which, during a retreat and combat of nearly five hours, never allowed the enemy to strike with its main force. Finally, all our troops began to march, and the Turks, constantly increasing in numbers, pursued us.

The same day, at noon, we were obliged to stop to rest and get water near the Pruth because of the great heat and of the fatigue of the troops, especially the Preobrazhensky Regiment which was constantly harassed by the enemy. . . . Meanwhile, the Turks assembled their whole army, including a certain number of Swedes, Poles, and Cossacks who had joined them at Bender. The Swedish Generals Sparr and Poniatowsky went to the Vizier Mahomet-Pasha and asked him what he was going to do. He answered that he intended to attack the retreating enemy. They then begged him to change his plan and merely to harass the Russian troops from all sides and to close all the routes, so that finally they might attack a weakened and weary army. The Vizier responded that he saw no reason to drag things out, and since there were very few Russians, they could be easily beaten. But the Swedes replied that numbers mattered very little, since the Russians were regular troops; the Turkish soldiers would not bear up under their fire, would lose courage, and be rendered ineffective. The Vizier grew angry and bitterly refused their advice; instead he assembled the *Janissaries* and the infantry, about 100,000 men, and the cavalry, about 120,000 without the Tartars. This formidable army furiously attacked the Russians three hours before sundown. . . . But, since they attacked us in one specific place and since we could observe that they were not mounting another attack, we were able to repulse their attack with fresh troops. . . .

2
Petrine Decrees

The decrees of Peter the Great embodied both the substance of the new era and the personality of the tsar himself, for the edicts always contained both the content of reform and educational exhortation from the tsar. A distinguished historian of Russian literature, Prince D. S. Mirsky, wrote:

Of all the original writings of the period, those of Peter himself are easily the best. His Russian was quaintly mixed with barbarisms, but he used it with vigor, terseness, and originality. His literary originality is evident everywhere—in his journals, in his letters, even, and perhaps best of all, in his official ordinances. The vivid and realistic imagery of his styles makes his ukases [decrees] the most enjoyable literature of the time. He had a genius for pithy and memorable statement, and many of his statements still live in everyone's memory.[1]

PETER'S PREFACE TO THE MARITIME REGULATIONS (1700)[2]

Peter here refers to himself in the third person.

On this account he turned his whole mind to the construction of a fleet, and when, on account of the Tartar insults, the siege of Azov was begun, and afterwards that town was fortunately taken, then, according to his unchangeable will, he did not endure thinking long about it. He quickly set about the work. A suitable place for shipbuilding was found on the river Voronezh, close to the town of that name, skilful ship-wrights were called from England and Holland, and in 1696 there began a new work in Russia—the construction of great war-ships, galleys, and other vessels; and so that this might be for ever secured in Russia, and that he might introduce among his people the

---

[1] D. S. Mirsky, *A History of Russian Literature from Its Beginning to 1900* (New York: Random House, Inc., 1958), p. 34.

[2] Eugene Schuyler, *Peter the Great, Emperor of Russia* (London: Sampson Low, Marston, Searle and Rivington, 1884), vol. 1, pp. 324–25.

art of this business, he sent many people of noble families to Holland and other states to learn the building and management of ships; and that the monarch might not be shamefully behind his subjects in that trade, he himself undertook a journey to Holland; and in Amsterdam, at the East India wharf, giving himself up, with other volunteers, to the learning of naval architecture, he got what was necessary for a good carpenter to know, and, by his own work and skill, constructed and launched a new ship.

DECREE ON THE INVITATION TO FOREIGNERS (APRIL 27, 1702)[3]

It is sufficiently known in all the lands which the Almighty has placed under our rule, that since our accession to the throne all our efforts and intentions have tended to govern this realm in such a way that all of our subjects should, through our care for the general good, become more and more prosperous. For this end we have always tried to maintain internal order, to defend the State against invasion, and in every possible way to improve and to extend trade. With this purpose we have been compelled to make some necessary and salutary changes in the administration, in order that our subjects might more easily gain a knowledge of matters of which they were before ignorant, and become more skilful in their commercial relations. We have therefore given orders, made dispositions, and founded institutions indispensable for increasing our trade with foreigners, and shall do the same in future. Nevertheless we fear that matters are not in such a good condition as we desire, and that our subjects cannot in perfect quietness enjoy the fruits of our labours, and we have therefore considered still other means to protect our frontier from the invasion of the enemy, and to preserve the rights and privileges of our State, and the general peace of all Christians, as is incumbent on a Christian monarch to do. To attain these worthy aims, we have endeavoured to improve our military forces, which are the protection of our State, so that our troops may consist of well-drilled men, maintained in perfect order and discipline. In order to obtain greater improvement in this respect, and to encourage foreigners, who are able to assist us in this way, as well as artists and artisans profitable to the State, to come in numbers to our country, we have issued this manifesto, and have ordered printed copies of it to be sent throughout Europe. And as in our residence of Moscow, the free exercise of religion of all other sects, although not agreeing with our church, is already allowed, so shall this be hereby confirmed

[3] Schuyler, *Peter the Great*, vol. 2, pp. 176–77.

anew in such wise that we, by the power granted to us by the Almighty, shall exercise no compulsion over the consciences of men, and shall gladly allow every Christian to care for his own salvation at his own risk.

THREE DECREES ON THE BUILDING OF SAINT PETERSBURG (1714)[4]

1. On the City Island and the Admiralty Island in Saint Petersburg, as likewise on the banks of the greater Neva and its more important arms, wooden buildings are forbidden, only adobe houses being allowed. The two above-mentioned islands and the embankments excepted, wood may be used for buildings, the plans to be obtained from the architect Trezzini. The roofs are to be covered either with two thicknesses of turf laid on rafters with cross-ribs (not on laths or boards), or with tiles. No other roof covering is allowed under penalty of severe fines. The streets should be bordered directly by the houses, not with fences or stables.

2. The most illustrious and mighty Peter the Great, Emperor and Autocrat of all Russia, has commanded his imperial decree to be proclaimed to people of all ranks. Whereas stone construction here is advancing very slowly, it being difficult to obtain stone-masons and other artisans of this craft even for good pay; for this reason all stone buildings of any description are forbidden in the whole state for a few years, until construction has sufficiently progressed here, under penalty of confiscation of the offender's property and exile. This decree is to be announced in all the cities and districts of the Saint Petersburg province, except this city, so that none may plead ignorance as an excuse.

3. The following is ordered: no building shall be undertaken in Petersburg on the grounds of houses, between neighboring back yards, until all the main and side streets are entirely built up. However, if after this any person needs more buildings, he may build on his grounds, along the neighbor's lot. No stables or barns may be built facing the street, but only inside the grounds. Along the streets and side streets all the space must be filled by residences, as ordered. In the locations where, as ordered by previous decrees, wooden houses may be built, they must be made of squared logs. If the logs are used as they are, the walls must be faced with boards and coated with red, or painted to look like brick.

[4] Reprinted from Marthe Blinoff, ed., *Life and Thought in Old Russia* (University Park: The Pennsylvania State University Press, 1961), pp. 16–17. Reprinted by permission of the publisher.

DECREE ON THE INTRODUCTION OF THE NEW CALENDAR (DECEMBER 20, 1699)[5]

His Majesty has ordered the following to be proclaimed: It is known to His Majesty that not only many European Christian lands, but also Slavic nations which are in total accord with our Eastern Orthodox Church, such as Vallachians, Moldavians, Serbs, Dalmatians, Bulgarians, and His Majesty's own subjects the Circassians, and all the Greeks, from whom we have received our faith—all those nations agree to count their years from the eighth day after the birth of Christ, that is from the first day of January, and not from the creation of the world,[6] because of the many difficulties and discrepancies of this reckoning. It is now the year 1699 from the birth of Christ, and from the first of January will begin both the new year 1700 and a new century; and so His Majesty has ordered, as a good and useful measure, that from now on time will be reckoned in government offices and dates to be noted on documents and property deeds, starting from the first of January 1700. And to celebrate this good undertaking and the new century, the following is ordered: in the sovereign city of Moscow, after due thanks and praise to God in the churches, or, as the case may be, at home, let the reputable citizens arrange decorations of pine, fir and juniper trees and boughs along the busiest main streets and by the houses of eminent church and lay persons of rank. These decorations may follow the pattern of those set up in the Merchant Court or near the Lower Pharmacy, or they may be disposed in the way most convenient and fitting to the various places and gates. Poorer persons should place at least one shrub or bough on their gates or on their house. All this should be made ready by the first of January, and remain in place until the seventh of January, 1700. Also, on the first day of January, as a sign of rejoicing, wishes for the new year and century will be exchanged, and the following will be organized: when fireworks are lit and guns fired on the great Red Square, let the boyars, the Lords of the Palace, of the Chamber, and the Council, and the eminent personages of Court, Army, and Merchant ranks, each in his own grounds, fire three times from small guns, if they have any, or from muskets and other small arms, and shoot some rockets into the air.

[5] Reprinted in Marthe Blinoff, ed., *Life and Thought in Old Russia* (University Park: The Pennsylvania State University Press, 1961), pp. 49–50. Reprinted by permission of the publisher.

[6] Before January 1, 1700, the Russian calendar was dated from the creation of the world, and began its year on September 1.

DECREES ON THE DUTIES OF THE SENATE⁷

This *ukaz* [decree] should be made known. We have decreed that during our absence administration of the country is to be [in the hands of] the Governing Senate [consisting of the following persons]: Count Musin-Pushkin, *gospodin* [Lord] Strezhnev, Prince Peter Golitsyn, Prince Michael Dolgoruky, *gospodin* Plemiannikov, Prince Gregory Volkonskii, *gospodin* Samarin, *gospodin* Vasili Opukhtin, [and] *gospodin* Melnitskii. Anisim Shchukin [is to act as] the Senate's Chief Secretary. Vasili Enhov is to administer the Moscow Gubernia [administrative unit] and to report [on it] to the Senate; the position of Prince Peter Golitsyn is to go to *gospodin* Kurbatov. The Military *prikaz* [department] is to be replaced by a Military Board [and is to be] attached to the above mentioned Senate.

Each *gubernia* is to send two officials to advise the Senate on judicial and legislative matters. . . .

In our absence the Senate is charged by this *ukaz* with the following:

1. To establish a just court, to deprive unjust judges of their offices and of all their property, and to administer the same treatment to all slanderers.

2. To supervise governmental expenditures throughout the country and cancel unnecessary and, above all, useless things.

3. To collect as much money as possible because money is the artery of war.

4. To recruit young noblemen for officer training, especially those who try to evade it; also to select about 1000 educated boyars for the same purpose.

5. To reform letters of exchange and keep these in one place.

6. To take inventory of goods leased to offices or *gubernias*.

7. To farm out the salt trade in an effort to receive some profit [for the state].

8. To organize a good company and assign to it the China trade.

9. To increase trade with Persia and by all possible means to attract in great numbers Armenians [to that trade]. To organize inspectors and inform them of their responsibilities.

⁷ "Decrees on the Duties of the Senate" and the following "Decrees on Compulsory Education of the Russian Nobility," "A Decree on Primogeniture," "An Instruction to Russian Students Abroad Studying Navigation," "A Decree on the Right of Factories to Buy Villages," "Table of Ranks," "A Decree on the Founding of the Academy," and "Peter I's Decree Against Peasant Flights," are reprinted from Basil Dmytryshyn, ed., *Imperial Russia: A Source Book 1700–1917* (New York: Holt, Rinehart and Winston, Inc., 1967), pp. 15–23, 116–17. Copyright © 1967 by Holt, Rinehart and Winston, Inc. Reprinted by permission of the publisher.

DECREES ON COMPULSORY EDUCATION
OF THE RUSSIAN NOBILITY, JANUARY 12,
AND FEBRUARY 28, 1714

Send to every *gubernia* some persons from mathematical schools to teach the children of the nobility—except those of freeholders and government clerks—mathematics and geometry; as a penalty [for evasion] establish a rule that no one will be allowed to marry unless he learns these [subjects]. Inform all prelates to issue no marriage certificates to those who are ordered to go to schools. . . .

The Great Sovereign has decreed: in all *gubernias* children between the ages of ten and fifteen of the nobility, of government clerks, and of lesser officials, except those of freeholders, must be taught mathematics and some geometry. Toward that end, students should be sent from mathematical schools [as teachers], several into each *gubernia*, to prelates and to renowned monasteries to establish schools. During their instruction these teachers should be given food and financial remuneration of three *altyns* and two *dengas*[8] per day from *gubernia* revenues set aside for that purpose by personal orders of His Imperial Majesty. No fees should be collected from students. When they have mastered the material, they should then be given certificates written in their own handwriting. When the students are released they ought to pay one ruble each for their training. Without these certificates they should not be allowed to marry nor receive marriage certificates.

A DECREE ON PRIMOGENITURE, MARCH 23, 1714

We, Peter I, Tsar and Autocrat of All Russia, etc., issue this *ukaz* for the knowledge of all subjects of our state, regardless of their social status.

The division of estates upon the death of the father causes great harm to our state and state interests and brings ruin to subjects and the families concerned; namely:

1. *On Taxes.* A man, for instance, had 1000 households and five sons, had a fine manor, good food, and a sound relationship with the people; if after his death this property is divided among his children, each would receive 200 households; those children, remembering the fame of their father and the honor of their family, would not wish to live the life of an orphan; everyone can see that poor subjects will have to supply five instead of one table, and 200 households cannot carry

---

[8] One *altyn* equalled six *dengas*, or three copecks; one *denga* equalled one-half copeck.—Ed.

the burden previously carried by 1000 (including state taxes). Does not this practice bring ruin to the people and harm to state interests? Because 200 households cannot pay as punctually to the state and to the nobleman as was possible from 1000 households, because (as noted above) one lord will be satisfied with 1000 (but not with 200) and the peasants, having better conditions, will be able to pay taxes punctually both to the state and to the lord. Consequently, division of estates brings great harm to the government treasury and ruin to subject people.

2. *On Families.* And should each of those five sons have two sons, each son will receive 100 households, and should they further multiply, they will be so impoverished that they may turn into one-household owners, with the result that [the descendants of] a famous family, in place of fame, will turn into villagers, a problem which has often occurred among the Russians.

3. On top of these two harmful practices, there is yet another problem. Anyone who receives his bread gratuitously, regardless of its amount, will neither serve the state without compulsion nor try to improve his conditions: on the contrary, each will try to live in idleness, which (according to Holy Scripture) is the mother of all evil.

In contrast to Item 1 [On Taxes]: if all immovable property were to be handed down to one son and the others were to inherit only movable property, then state revenues would be sounder; the nobleman would be better off even if he should collect small amounts [from his subjects]; there will be only one manor (as stated above); and his subjects will not be ruined.

Regarding Item 2 [On Families]: families will not decline, but shall remain stable in all their glory and their manors shall remain famous and renowned.

Regarding Item 3: the remaining [members of the family] will not be idle because they will be forced to earn a living through service, teaching, trade, and so forth. And whatever they do for their own living will also benefit the state. Because this [system] is intended to bring prosperity, the following rules should be followed:

(a) All immovable property, namely hereditary, service, and purchased estates, as well as homes and stores, should neither be sold nor mortgaged but retained in the family in the following manner:

(b) Whoever has sons must will his immovable property to one who will inherit all; other children of both sexes will be rewarded by movable property which either the father or mother will divide for both sons and daughters in the amount they wish, except that the one who inherits the immovable property [will be excluded]. If an individual does not have sons, but daughters only, he should then divide [his property] in the same manner. If an individual fails to assign [his property] a government decree will assign the immovable property to the eldest son in inheritance, while movable property will be divided equally among the others; the same procedure is to apply to daughters.

(c) Whoever is childless will give his immovable property to one of the members of his family, whomever he wishes, and the movable [property] to his relatives or even to strangers. And if he fails to do this, both of these properties will then be divided by a decree among the members of the family; immovable to the nearest member of the family and the rest to all others equally. . . .

AN INSTRUCTION TO RUSSIAN STUDENTS ABROAD STUDYING NAVIGATION

1. Learn [how to draw] plans and charts and how to use the compass and other naval indicators.

2. [Learn] how to navigate a vessel in battle as well as in a simple maneuver, and learn how to use all appropriate tools and instruments; namely, sails, ropes, and oars, and the like matters, on row boats and other vessels.

3. Discover as much as possible how to put ships to sea during a naval battle. Those who cannot succeed in this effort must diligently ascertain what action should be taken by the vessels that do and those that do not put to sea during such a situation [naval battle]. Obtain from [foreign] naval officers written statements, bearing their signatures and seals, of how adequately you [Russian students] are prepared for [naval] duties.

4. If, upon his return, anyone wishes to receive [from the Tsar] greater favors for himself, he should learn, in addition to the above enumerated instructions, how to construct those vessels aboard which he would like to demonstrate his skills.

5. Upon his return to Moscow, every [foreign-trained Russian] should bring with him at his own expense, for which he will later be reimbursed, at least two experienced masters of naval science. They [the returnees] will be assigned soldiers, one soldier per returnee, to teach them [what they have learned abroad]. And if they do not wish to accept soldiers they may teach their acquaintances or their own people. The treasury will pay for transportation and maintenance of soldiers. And if anyone other than soldiers learns [the art of navigation] the treasury will pay 100 rubles for the maintenance of every such individual. . . .

A DECREE ON THE RIGHT OF FACTORIES
TO BUY VILLAGES, JANUARY 18, 1721

Previous decrees have denied merchants the right to obtain villages. This prohibition was instituted because those people, outside their business, did not have any establishments that could be of any use to the state. Nowadays, thanks to our decrees, as every one can see, many merchants have companies and many have succeeded in establishing new enterprises for the benefit of the state; namely: silver, copper, iron, coal and the like, as well as silk, linen, and woolen industries, many of which have begun operations. As a result, by this our *ukaz* aimed at the increase of factories, we permit the nobility as well as merchants to freely purchase villages for these factories, with the sanction of the Mining and Manufacturing College, under one condition: that these villages be always integral parts of these factories. Consequently, neither the nobility nor merchants may sell or mortgage these villages without the factories . . . and should someone decide to sell these villages with the factories because of pressing needs, it must be done with the permission of the Mining and Manufacturing College. And whoever violates this procedure will have his possessions confiscated.

And should someone try to establish a small factory for the sake of appearance in order to purchase a village, such an entrepreneur should not be allowed to purchase anything. The Mining and Manufacturing College should adhere to this rule very strictly. Should such a thing happen, those responsible for it should be deprived of all their movable and immovable property.

TABLE OF RANKS, JANUARY 24, 1722

Military Ranks		Civilian Ranks	Grades
Naval Forces	Land Forces		
General-Admiral	Generalissimo Field Marshal	Chancelor or Active Privy Counselor	I
Admiral	General of Artillery General of Cavalry General of Infantry	Active Privy Counselor	II
Vice Admiral	Lieutenant General	Privy Counselor	III
Rear Admiral	Major General	Active State Counselor	IV
Captain-Commander	Brigadier	State Counselor	V
First Captain	Colonel	Collegial Counselor	VI

Second Captain	Lieutenant Colonel	Court Counselor	VII
Lieutenant-Captain of the Fleet	Major	Collegial Assessor	VIII
Third Captain of Artillery			
Lieutenant of the Fleet	Captain or Cavalry Captain	Titled Counselor	IX
Lieutenant-Captain of Artillery			
Lieutenant of Artillery	Staff Captain or Staff Cavalry Captain	Collegial Secretary	X
		Secretary of the Senate	XI
Midshipman	Lieutenant	*Gubernia* Secretary	XII
Artillery Constable	Sublieutenant	Registrar of the Senate	XIII
	Guidon Bearer	Collegial Registrar	XIV

The following rules are appended to the above Table of Ranks to inform everyone of how he should apply himself to these ranks.

1. Those princes who are related to Us by blood or those who are married to Our princesses always take precedence and rank over all other princes and high servants of the Russian state.

2. Naval and land commanding officers are to be determined in the following manner: if they both are of the same rank, the naval officer is superior at sea to the land officer, and on land, the land officer is superior to the naval officer, regardless of the length of service each may have in his respective rank.

3. Whoever shall demand respect higher than is due his rank, or shall illegally assume a higher rank, shall lose two months of his salary; if he serves without salary then he shall pay a fine equal to the salary of his rank; one third of that fine shall be given to the individual who reported on him, and the remainder will be given to a hospital fund. The observance of this rank procedure does not apply on such occasions as meetings among friends or neighbors or at social gatherings, but only to churches, the Mass, Court ceremonies, ambassadorial audiences, official banquets, official meetings, christenings, marriages, funerals, and similar public gatherings. An individual will also be fined if he should make room for a person of lower rank. Tax collectors should watch carefully [for any signs of violations of these procedures] in order to encourage service [to the state] and to honor those already in service, and [at the same time] to collect fines from im-

pudent individuals and parasites. The above prescribed fines are applicable to male and female transgressors.

4. An identical penalty will be given to anyone who will demand a rank without having an appropriate patent for his grade.

5. Equally, no one may assume a rank that has been acquired in the service of a foreign state until We approve it, an action which We shall do gladly in accordance with his service.

6. No one may be given a new rank without a release patent, unless We personally have signed that release.

7. All married women advance in ranks with their husbands, and if they should violate the order of procedure they must pay the same fines as would their husbands if they had violated it.

8. Although We allow free entry to public assemblies, wherever the Court is present, to the sons of princes, counts, barons, distinguished nobles, and high servants of the Russian state, either because of their births or because of the positions of their fathers, and although We wish to see that they are distinguished in every way from other [people], We nevertheless do not grant any rank to anyone until he performs a useful service to Us or to the state. . . .

11. All Russian or foreign-born servants who have or who have had the first eight grades have the right forever to pass these grades on to their lawful heirs and posterity; members of ancient [Russian] noble families, even though they may be of lesser status and may never before have been brought into a noble dignity by the Crown or granted a coat of arms, should be given the same merits and preferences [as other nobles]. . . .

15. Those who are not nobles but who serve in the military and who advance to an *ober*-officer [position], will, upon attainment of that rank, receive the status of a nobleman, as will those of their children born *ex post facto*. In case an individual has no children after becoming an *ober*-officer, but has children born earlier, he may petition the Tsar, and the status of a nobleman will be granted to one son in whose behalf the father has petitioned. Children of all other grades whose parents are not nobles, regardless of whether they serve in civil or Court positions, are not considered as nobles. . . .

A DECREE ON THE FOUNDING OF THE ACADEMY, JANUARY 28, 1724

His Imperial Majesty decreed the establishment of an academy, wherein languages as well as other sciences and important arts could be taught, and where books could be translated. On January 22, [1724], during his stay in the Winter Palace, His Majesty approved the project for the Academy, and with his own hand signed a decree that stipulates that the Academy's budget of 24,912 rubles annually should come from revenues from custom dues and export-import license fees collected in the following cities: Narva, Dorpat, Pernov and Arensburg. . . .

Usually two kinds of institutions are used in organizing arts and sciences. One is known as a University; the other as an Academy or society of arts and sciences.

1. A University is an association of learned individuals who teach the young people the development of such distinguished sciences as theology and jurisprudence (the legal skill), and medicine and philosophy. An Academy, on the other hand, is an association of learned and skilled people who not only know their subjects to the same degree [as their counterparts in the University] but who, in addition, improve and develop them through research and inventions. They have no obligation to teach others.

2. While the Academy consists of the same scientific disciplines and has the same members as the University, these two institutions, in other states, have no connection between themselves in training many other well-qualified people who could organize different societies. This is done to prevent interference into the activity of the Academy, whose sole task is to improve arts and sciences through theoretical research that would benefit professors as well as students of universities. Freed from the pressure of research, universities can concentrate on educating the young people.

3. Now that an institution aimed at the cultivation of arts and sciences is to be chartered in Russia, there is no need to follow the practice that is accepted in other states. It is essential to take into account the existing circumstances of this state [Russia], consider [the quality of Russian] teachers and students, and organize such an institution that would not only immediately increase the glory of this [Russian] state through the development of sciences, but would also, through teaching and dissemination [of knowledge], benefit the people [of Russia] in the future.

4. These two aims will not be realized if the Academy of Sciences alone is chartered, because while the Academy may try to promote and disseminate arts and sciences, these will not spread among the people. The establishment of a university will do even less, simply because there are no elementary schools, gymnasia or seminaries [in Russia] where young people could learn the fundamentals before studying more advanced subjects [at the University] to make themselves useful. It is therefore inconceivable that under these circumstances a university would be of some value [to Russia].

5. Consequently what is needed most [in Russia] is the establishment

of an institution that would consist of the most learned people, who, in turn, would be willing: (a) to promote and perfect the sciences while at the same time, wherever possible, be willing (b) to give public instruction to young people (if they feel the latter are qualified) and (c) instruct some people individually so that they in turn could train young people [of Russia] in the fundamental principles of all sciences.

6. As a result, and with only slight modifications, one institution will perform as great a service [in Russia] as the three institutions do in other states. . . .

7. Because the organization of this Academy is similar to that of Paris (except for this difference and advantage that the Russian Academy is also to do what a university and college are doing [in Paris]), I think that this institution can and should easily be called an Academy. Disciplines which can be organized in this Academy can easily be grouped in three basic divisions: The first division is to consist of mathematical and related sciences; the second of physics; and the third of humanities, history and law. . . .

PETER I'S DECREE AGAINST PEASANT FLIGHTS, APRIL 5, 1707

Last year, 1706, fugitives and peasants appeared in Moscow and other cities; on settlements, crown villages and on the estates of the patriarch, bishops, monasteries, church and other clergy; these fugitives and peasants, with their wives, children, and belongings, should be returned to their previous *pomeshchiks* and *votchinniks* from whom they fled within half a year from the date of this *ukaz*. Whoever retains these fugitives and peasants beyond that date and will not return them to their rightful owners will lose half of his estate to the Great Sovereign, the other half going to those to whom the fugitives or peasants belong. And should those fugitives and peasants who were sent to their original places be unable to reach them because of interference by other nobles, stewards, elders, or peasants who would like to have them for themselves, should this be established beyond doubt, then . . . this will be contrary to the sovereign's *ukaz*. The great sovereign was informed this year, 1707, that many nobles have lost the fear of God, have overlooked the *ukaz* of the Great Sovereign, and have kept the fugitives and peasants and sent other people away from their estates, but not to the original places; while some nobles do not allow them [the fugitives] to reach their destination by taking them in. The Great Sovereign, Peter Alekseevich, Tsar and Grand Prince, autocrat of all Great, Little and White Russia, by this personal *ukaz* orders that these nobles, stewards and elders who keep the old fugitives and peasants, or who take on new ones, or do not return them to their rightful destination . . . will be punished without delay. *Voevodas* [administrative leaders] should go into villages and collect information from nobles, stewards, and elders as to whether they have fulfilled their duties or not; and in each small village they should collect from five to six, and in large [villages] from ten to fifteen, good respectable men, testimony sworn on the penalty of death about the above mentioned fugitive peasants. Copies of this *ukaz* of the Great Sovereign should be posted on all gates, and be distributed in cities and offices for everyone to remember.

THE PEACE OF NYSTADT, 1721[9]

Strictly speaking, Tsar Peter did not write the Peace of Nystadt, but historically speaking the treaty was created by Peter's ambition and his energy, and represents the culmination of his work. The cession of the Baltic coastline, for which Peter had fought for over twenty years, was guaranteed by this treaty.

In the name of the Very Holy and Indivisible Trinity, be it known by this treaty that, as there has been carried on for several years a bloody, long and difficult war between His Majesty the dead King Charles XII, of glorious memory, King of Sweden, . . . and his successor to the throne of Sweden, Ulrica, Queen of Sweden . . . , and, on the other hand, His Czarist Majesty Peter I, Emperor of all Russia . . . , the two parties have found the means to conclude these troubles, and consequently put an end to the shedding of so much innocent blood. It has pleased Divine Providence to dispose the minds of the two sides to assemble their ministers plenipotentiary in order to conclude a firm, sincere, and stable peace and an eternal friendship between the two states, provinces, vassals, subjects and inhabitants. . . .

Article I. There will be from this moment and forever an inviolable peace on land and sea and a sincere, friendly and indissoluble union between His Majesty King Frederick I, King of Sweden, etc., his successors to the crown and the Kingdom of Sweden, and all his domains, provinces, cities, vassals, subjects and inhabitants, and His Czarist Majesty Peter I, Emperor of all Russia, etc., his successors to the throne of Russia, and all his provinces, cities, vassals, subjects and inhabitants. . . . In the future the two peaceful parties will not commit, nor permit to be committed, any secret or public, direct or indirect hostility either by themselves or by others. They will give aid

[9] Reprinted in Voltaire, "Histoire de l'empire de Russie sous Pierre le Grand," *Oeuvres complètes de Voltaire* (Paris: 1878), vol. 16, pp. 630–38; trans. L. J. Oliva.

to no enemy of either of the two peaceful parties under any pretext whatever and will make no alliance which would be contrary to this peace. They will continue always between themselves a sincere friendship and will try to maintain honor and mutual security. They will also try to avoid, as much as possible, damages and troubles with which both parties could be threatened by some other power. . . .

Article IV. His Majesty, the King of Sweden, by the present articles, cedes for himself and for his successors in the Kingdom of Sweden, to His Czarist Majesty and his successors in the Russian empire, in full, irrevocable and eternal possession, the provinces which have been conquered and taken by the arms of His Czarist Majesty in this war against the crown of Sweden. That is to say: Livonia, Estonia, Ingria, and part of Karelia as far as the district of Vibourg which is specified below in the article on boundaries, the cities and fortresses of Riga, Dunemund, Pernau, Reval, Dorpat, Narva, Vibourg, Kexholm, and other cities, fortresses, ports, places, districts, coasts and rivers pertaining to the said provinces, as also the isles of Oesel, Daghoe, Moen, and all the other islands along the frontier of Courland and along the coasts of Livonia, Estonia, and Ingria, and on the western side of Reval, . . . with all the inhabitants who find themselves in these islands and in foresaid provinces, cities, and places, and generally all their appurtenances, dependencies, prerogatives, rights, and emoluments, without any exception, which the crown of Sweden has possessed.

In order to effect this, His Majesty the King of Sweden renounces forever in a most solemn manner for himself and for his successors and for the whole Kingdom of Sweden, all claims that he has had up to this time or could have, on the aforesaid provinces, islands, countries and places, all of whose inhabitants will be, in virtue of the present treaty, discharged from the oath that they have taken to the crown of Sweden. His Majesty and the Kingdom of Sweden will demand allegiance of them no more nor ask it of them forever under any pretext whatever, but they will be and will remain incorporated in perpetuity in the Russian empire. And His Majesty and the Kingdom of Sweden will engage by the present treaty always to help maintain His Czarist Majesty and his successors in the Russian empire in the peaceful possession of these provinces, islands, places, and districts. And they will seek and will return to those who will be authorized by His Czarist Majesty all the archives and papers which have been taken and carried to Sweden during this war, which principally concern these countries.

Article V. His Czarist Majesty promises His Majesty and the crown of Sweden in return to restore and to evacuate within four weeks after the exchange of ratifications of this peace treaty, or sooner if possible, the Grand Duchy of Finland, except the part which has been reserved below in the boundary details, which will belong to His Czarist Majesty. His Czarist Majesty and his successors will not have claim nor will they ever make any claims on the said Duchy, under any pretext whatever. His Czarist Majesty engages and promises to pay promptly and without rebate the sum of 2 million *ecus* to the authorities of the King of Sweden, providing that they produce and give the above mentioned agreements in the terms described. . . .

Article VII. His Czarist Majesty also promises, in the manner most solemn, that he will not mingle in the domestic affairs of the Kingdom of Sweden nor the form of regency which has been regulated and established unanimously by the estates of the foresaid Kingdom; that he will not assist anyone in any manner directly or indirectly who tries to prevent or to carry out what is contrary. . . . He will give clear marks of sincere friendship and true neighborliness. . . .

Article IX. His Czarist Majesty promises to maintain all the inhabitants of the provinces of Livonia, Estonia, and Oesel, nobles and free peasants, magistrates and artisans, in the entire enjoyment of the customary privileges and prerogatives which they have enjoyed under the rule of the King of Sweden.

Article X. One will not introduce restraints of conscience in the countries which have been ceded, but one will allow and maintain the evangelical religion as well as the churches and the schools and their dependencies on the same footing as they were in the time of the last regency of the King of Sweden, on the condition that the Greek religion is also freely exercised.

Made at Nystadt, August 30th, 1721.

3
Peter and His Family

Peter's relationship to his mother was an ambivalent one. Throughout his youth, she was the ambitious manager of his future when he seemed incapable of or uninterested in managing his own. She was staid and conservative, but tough and determined; she disapproved of Peter's amusements, of his carousing with foreigners, and of his military and naval escapades, but Peter depended heavily on her until her death in 1694. In the first letter, Peter is refusing to come to Moscow to attend a mass in honor of the dead Tsar Fyodor, and in the rest he is fending off her insistence that he give up his shipbuilding and come home.

August 21, 1693

Thou hast written, O lady! that I have saddened thee by not writing of my arrival. But even now I have no time to write in detail, because I am expecting some ships, and as soon as they come—when no one knows, but they are expected soon, as they are more than three weeks from Amsterdam—I shall come to thee immediately, travelling day and night. But I beg thy mercy for one thing: why dost thou trouble thyself about me? Thou hast deigned to write that thou hast given me into the care of the Virgin. When thou hast such a guardian for me, why dost thou grieve?

By thy letter I see, Oh! Oh! that thou hast been mightily grieved, and why? If thou art grieved, what delight have I? I beg thee make my wretched self happy by not grieving about me, for in very truth I cannot endure it.

September 18, 1693

Thou hast deigned to write to me, O my delight! to say that I should write to thee oftener. Even now I write by every post, and my

[1] The following letters from Peter to Natalia are reprinted from Schuyler, *Peter the Great*, vol. 1, pp. 145–47, 277–78.

only fault is that I do not come myself. And thou also tellest me not to get ill by too quick a journey. But I, thank God! shall try not to get ill, except by coming too quickly. But thou makest me ill by thy grief, and the Hamburg ships have not yet arrived.

April 20, 1689

To my most beloved, and while bodily life endures my dearest little mother, Lady Tsaritsa and Grand-Duchess Natalia Kirilovna. Thy little son, now here at work, Petrushka, I ask thy blessing and desire to hear about thy health, and we, through thy prayers, are all well, and the lake is all got clear from the ice today, and all the boats, except the big ship, are finished, only we are waiting for ropes, and therefore I beg your kindness that these ropes, seven hundred fathoms long, be sent from the Artillery Department without delaying, for the work is waiting for them, and our sojourn here is being prolonged. For this I ask your blessing. From Pereyaslavl.

April 30, 1689

To my most beloved and dearest mother, Lady Tsaritsa Natalia Kirilovna, thy unworthy son, Petrushka, I desire greatly to know about thy health; and as to what thou hast done in ordering me go to Moscow, I am ready, only, hey! hey! there is work here, and the man you sent has seen it himself, and will explain more clearly; and we, through thy prayers, are in perfect health. About my coming I have written more extendedly to Leo Kirilovitch, and he will report to thee, O lady. Therefore, I must humbly surrender myself to your will. Amen.

May 1689

To my dearest Mother, I, the unworthy Petrushka, asking thy blessing, petition. For thy message by the Doctor and Gabriel, I rejoice, just as Noah did once over the olive-branch. Through thy prayers we are all in good health, and the boats have succeeded all mighty well. For this may the Lord grant thee health, both in soul and body, just as I wish.

May 1689

Hey! I wish to hear about thy health, and beg thy blessing. We are all well: and about the boats, I say again that they are mighty good, and Tikhon Nikititch will tell you about all this himself. Thy unworthy Petrus.

PETER AND HIS SON, ALEXEI

Peter's son by his first wife, whom he divorced and immured in a convent in 1699, was Tsarevich Alexei. The boy grew to hate his father, and Peter could see nothing of promise for the future in his son. Alexei served more and more as a focus for those who were discontented with the reforms. Peter hoped to replace Alexei as his heir with a child by his second wife, and urged his son to surrender his right to the throne. Alexei, in fear of his father, fled to Austria and finally to Italy. He returned to Russia under guarantees of pardon from Peter, but was interrogated in order to implicate others and died under torture. Following are Peter's letters demanding Alexei's resignation, his letter urging Alexei's return from exile, the official condemnation decree of the tsarevich, and the Circular to Ambassadors announcing his death.

Peter to Alexei, Copenhagen, September 6, 1716 [2]

My Son—I have received your two letters of July 10 and August 10, in which you write only of your health. Wherefore I remind you by this letter.

When I bade you good-bye, and asked you about your resolution in a certain matter, you replied always one thing: that on account of your feebleness you were not fit for the inheritance, and wished rather to go into a monastery; then I told you to think this over seriously, and to write me what resolution you had taken, for which I have waited seven months. During all that time you have written nothing whatever about this matter. Therefore now, for you have had time enough for reflection, on the receipt of this letter immediately make a resolution for the first or the second. If you take the first, do not delay more than a week. Come here, for you can still get here in time for the campaign. If you take the second, write to me where and on what day, so that I may have peace in my conscience as to what I may expect of you. Send back this courier with the final answer. If the first, when you are going to leave Saint Petersburg; if the second, when you will fulfil it. I must now make sure that this be finally done, for I see that you are only wasting time in your usual idleness.

[2] Schuyler, *Peter the Great*, vol. 2, p. 407.

Peter to Alexei, Spa, July 21, 1717 [3]

My Son—It is known to everyone how you have been disobedient and
what contempt you have shown me, and how neither words nor
punishments have been able to make you follow my orders, at last
deceiving me and asking God to witness at your taking leave of me.
What have you done? You have run away and have put yourself, like
a traitor, under foreign protection—an unheard-of thing. By this
affront what grief you have caused your father, and what shame your
country! I therefore now send this last message to you that you may
act according to my will, as M. Tolstoi and M. Rumiantsof will tell
you. If you submit to me, I assure you—and I promise by God and
His Judgement—that you shall have no punishment, but I will show
you my best love if you are obedient and return. But if you refuse,
then, as a father, by the power given to me by God, I curse you
eternally; and, as your sovereign, I declare you a traitor, and I shall
leave unused no means of punishing you as a traitor and a reviler of
your father; in which may God help me in my right! Remember, besides, that I have done nothing to you forcibly, and if you only would,
all would have been according to your will. What you wish, that do.

The Condemnation of the Czarevich Alexei, June 24, 1718 [4]

By virtue of the order of His Czarist Majesty signed in his own
hand last June 13, ordering the trial of the Czarevich Alexei Petrovich
for his transgressions and crimes against his father and sovereign, the
undersigned ministers, Senators, and military and civil officials, have
met several times in the Senate chambers at Petersburg, have reviewed
several times the originals and extracts of testimony made against him
and also letters of exhortation from His Czarist Majesty to the Czarevich and the responses which are in his own hand, and other acts
pertaining to the trial such as criminal information and confession
and declarations of the Czarevich either written by him or made orally
to his father and sovereign. The undersigned appointed by His Czarist
Majesty have arrived at the following judgment. They recognize that
according to the laws of this empire the matter is not their affair since
they are all natural subjects of His Czarist Majesty, and recognize that
an important affair of this sort depends uniquely on the absolute will
of the sovereign whose power comes from God alone and is unlimited
by any law. Thus submitting ourselves to the order of His Czarist

[3] Schuyler, *Peter the Great*, vol. 2, p. 416.
[4] Voltaire, *"Histoire de l'empire de Russie,"* in *Oeuvres complètes de Voltaire* (Paris: Garnier Frères, 1878), vol. 16, pp. 627–30; trans. L. J. Oliva.

Majesty, our sovereign, who gives us this right, and after mature reflection and in Christian conscience without fear or flattery and without regard to any person, taking into account only the divine law as it applies in this case, the Old and the New Testaments, the Gospels and the writings of the Apostles, the decisions of the Church councils, the teachings of the fathers and the doctors of the Church, and taking also the advice of the leading Church dignitaries assembled at Petersburg by His Czarist Majesty, and in agreement with the laws of Russia and in particular the constitution of this empire, its military statutes which are similar to those of other states . . . the undersigned are unanimous in their judgment and pronounce that the Czarevich Alexei Petrovich is worthy of death for his crimes and sins against his father and sovereign, being both son and subject to His Czarist Majesty.

His Czarist Majesty had promised the Czarevich, by a letter which he had sent to him in care of Tolstoy, his Privy Counselor, and by Captain Romanzov, dated at Spa the 10th of July, 1717, to pardon him his transgressions if he returned willingly. The Czarevich gratefully acknowledged to him in his response to this letter, written from Naples on the 4th of October, 1717, that he was grateful to His Czarist Majesty for the pardon which had been given to him for his flight, that he was unworthy of such mercy because of his opposition to the will of his father and because of his other continually repeated sins. . . .

His Czarist Majesty, when the Czarevich arrived at Moscow with a written confession of his crimes and asked pardon, had pity on him as is natural for a father towards his son. In an audience with him given in the main hall of the palace on the same day, the 3rd of February, His Czarist Majesty promised him pardon for all his crimes on the express condition that he confess in the presence of everyone and that he declare, without any restriction or reserve, all that he had committed and done up to that day against His Czarist Majesty and that he reveal all the persons who had given him counsel, his accomplices, and generally all those who had known anything of his plans. If all of this were not done, the promised pardon would be null and void. The Czarevich received this and accepted it, at least in appearance, with tears of gratitude, and he promised by oath to hold back nothing. In confirmation of this he kissed the Holy Cross and the Holy Scriptures in the cathedral church.

His Czarist Majesty confirmed this arrangement in his own hand the next day, as contained in the articles of interrogation inserted below: "As you have yesterday received your pardon on condition that you declare all the circumstances of your flight and everything else there is to report, if you hide anything you will be deprived of your life. And as you have already made certain declarations orally, you must make ample satisfaction and discharge your obligations by putting them in writing according to the points listed."

And at the conclusion His Czarist Majesty wrote in his own hand in the seventh article: "Confess everything which relates to this affair, even those things which are not specified here, and purge yourself as in the holy confession; but if you hide or conceal anything which is discovered later on, then impute nothing to me, because it has been declared to you yesterday before all the world that in that case the pardon that you have received would be null and revoked."

Notwithstanding this, the Czarevich has displayed no sincerity in his responses and in his confessions. He has concealed not only persons but also capital offenses, in particular his plans of rebellion against his father and his sovereign and the designs which he has entertained for a long time to usurp the throne of his father, even while he lived, by different evil methods. He based his hopes on the expectation that he could cause the death of his lord and sovereign and declare that he was the choice of the people.

All this was discovered afterward through criminal informers; the Czarevich had refused to declare it himself as appears below.

Thus, it is evident from all these plots of the Czarevich and from the declarations that he gave in writing and orally, the last being given on the 22nd of June of the present year, that he has never desired that the succession to the throne pass to him normally after the death of his father, in the manner that his father would have wished to leave it to him according to the order of equity and by the ways and means which God has prescribed. Instead, he has desired and planned to seize the throne, during the lifetime of his lord and father, against the will of His Czarist Majesty and in opposition to all that his father desired, not only by inciting uprisings and rebellions but also by securing the assistance of the emperor and a foreign army which he sought to have at his disposition, even at the cost of the overthrow of the state and the loss of all the state's achievements.

The Czarevich, in hiding all these evil plans and in concealing the persons who have been the instigators behind him as he has done right up to the last questioning, has planned to preserve some of his resources for the future when a favorable occasion might present itself for him to undertake his plans again and to push to a conclusion the execution of this horrible enterprise against his father and lord and against all this empire.

He has made himself unworthy of the clemency and pardon which was promised to him by his lord and father. He has said so himself before His Czarist Majesty and in the presence of all the ecclesiastics and secular lords, and publicly before all assembled. And he has also declared it verbally and in writing before the undersigned judges, established by His Czarist Majesty, and it is amply demonstrated by the evidence provided.

Thus, the divine and ecclesiastical laws, the civil and military regulations, and particularly the last two, condemn to death without mercy those whose attacks against their father and lord have been shown by evidence or proved by writing; they also condemn those who have only intended to rebel, or who have simply formed plans to kill their sovereign or usurp the empire, or who only contemplate such a plan or rebellion, which has not even been uttered in public. The Czarevich contemplated a horrible double parricide against his lord: first against the father of his country and second against his own natural father, a very clement father who has raised the Czarevich since his infancy with the most paternal care and with a tenderness and a goodness which have always been recognized. The father tried to educate the son for government, and to instruct him carefully in the important military arts in order to make him capable and worthy of succession to such a great empire. How much more reason that such an evil plan merits punishment by death.

It is with an afflicted heart and tearful eyes that we, as servants and subjects, pronounce this sentence, knowing that it is really not in our province to make a judgment of such great importance and particularly to pronounce a sentence against the son of the great and most clement sovereign Czar, our lord. However, his will being that we make a judgment, we declare by this present decree our true opinion and we pronounce his condemnation with a conscience so pure and so Christian that we believe we can sustain it before the terrible, just, and impartial judgment of the great God.

We submit this sentence which we have rendered and this condemnation that we have made to the sovereign power, and to the will and to the merciful revision of His Czarist Majesty, our very merciful monarch.

Circular to Foreign Ambassadors, July 10, 1718 [5]

When we remained undecided about our feelings of paternal pity and the duty of guaranteeing the future of our empire, Almighty God, in his justice, charged himself to spare us this trial. He put an end yesterday to the days of our son Alexei. After the reading of the judgement which enumerated his crimes, this culpable son was struck by a cruel malady, quite similar at the beginning to an attack of apoplexy. Subsequently, having recovered consciousness and taken the sacrament, according to Christian rite, he asked for us. We went to him with

[5] Schuyler, *Peter the Great*, vol. 2, pp. 434-35.

our Ministers and senators. He then confessed freely all his crimes, addressed us with tears of repentance and solicited our pardon, which we paternally granted to him, after which he made a Christian end this same day, June 26 (July 7 N.S.) towards six o'clock in the evening.

PETER AND CATHERINE I⁶

Peter divorced his first wife, Eudoxia, in 1699, and married his second, Catherine, in 1710. Catherine Skavronsky had been taken prisoner on the Baltic Coast in the early stages of the Great Northern War, and had been passed through the ranks until she became the mistress of Alexander Menshikov. It was in Menshikov's house that Tsar Peter met this hard-drinking, buxom woman; he lived with her, married her, and had her crowned as his empress. They had a warm and close relationship, as can be seen from their letters. Catherine ruled after Peter's death, from 1725 to 1727.

Peter to Catherine

From Lublin, capital of Ivashka, August 31, 1709

Moeder, Since I went away from thee I have no news of what I want to know, and especially how soon thou wilt be in Wilna. I am bored without thee, and thou, I think, art the same. Here, thank God, all is well. King Augustus has come in, and Krassau has gone out; Leszczynski has let his beard grow because his crown has died out. The Poles are constantly in conference about the affairs of Ivashka Khmelnitsky [are carousing]. . . .

Warsaw, September 24, 1709

Thanks for thy package. I send thee some fresh lemons. Thou dost jest about amusements; we have none, for we are old, and not that kind of people. . . . Give my regards to Aunty. Her bridegroom had an interview day before yesterday with Ivashka (got drunk), and had a bad fall on the boat, and now lies powerless; which break gently to Aunty, that she do not go to pieces. . . .

⁶ The letters are from Schuyler, *Peter the Great*, vol. 1, pp. 539–44. The "Decree on the Coronation of Catherine" is from Voltaire, *Oeuvres*, vol. 16, p. 639; trans. L. J. Oliva.

Marienwerder, October 16, 1709

. . . Give my regards to Aunty. That she has fallen in love with a monk I have already told her bridegroom, about which he is very sad, and from grief wishes himself to commit some follies.

Carlsbad, September 14, 1711

Katerinushka, my friend, how art thou?

We arrived here well, thank God, and to-morrow begin our cure. This place is so merry, you might call it an honourable dungeon, for it lies between such high mountains that one scarcely sees the sun. Worst of all, there is no good beer. However, we hope God will give us good from the waters. I send thee herewith a present, a new-fashioned clock, put under glass on account of the dust, and a seal. . . . I couldn't get more on account of my hurry for I was only one day in Dresden.

Carlsbad, September 19, 1711

. . . We, thank God, are well, only our bellies are swelled up with water, because we drink like horses, and we have nothing else to do except. . . . You write that on account of the cure I should not hurry to you. It is quite evident that you have found somebody better than me. Kindly write about it. Is it one of ours or a man of Thorn? I rather think a man of Thorn, and that you want to be revenged for what I did two years ago. That is the way you daughters of Eve act with us old fellows.

Griefswald, August 2, 1712

. . . Thank God, we are well, only 'tis hard living, for can't use my left hand, and in my right alone I have to hold both sword and pen. How many helpers I have thou knowest.

Griefswald, August 8, 1712

I hear that thou art bored, and I am not without being bored, but thou canst judge that business does not leave me much time for ennui. I don't think I can get away from here to thee quickly; and if the horses have arrived, come on with the three battalions that are ordered to go to Anclam. But, for God's sake, take care not to go a hundred yards from the battalions, for there are many enemy's ships in the Haff, and the men constantly go into the woods in great numbers, and through those woods thou must pass.

Berlin, October 2, 1712

I inform you that day before yesterday I arrived here and went to see the King. Yesterday morning he came to me, and last night I went to the Queen. I send you as many oysters as I could find. I couldn't get any more, because they say the pest has broken out in Hamburg, and it is forbidden to bring anything from there.

Leipzig, October 6, 1712

I this moment start for Carlsbad, and hope to arrive to-morrow. Your clothes and other things were bought, but I couldn't get any oysters. With this I confide you to God's keeping.

Carlsbad, October 11, 1712

We began to drink water at this hole yesterday. How it works I shall write, but don't ask for any other news from this wilderness.

Lagau, December 2, 1712

. . . Thanks for the clothes, which I put on new on St. Andrew's Day. As to what you say about bringing you here, we must put that off for a while, for the time has come for you to pray and for us to work. The Swedes yesterday attacked the Danes to keep them from joining us, and we are starting this moment to help the Danes.

Leaving Altona, May 23, 1716

Katerinushka, my heart's friend, how are you? Thanks for the present. In the same way I send you something from here in return. Really on both sides the presents are suitable. You sent me wherewithal to help my old age, and I send you with which to adorn your youth.

Pyrmont, June 5, 1716

I received your letter with the present, and I think you have a prophetic spirit that you sent only one bottle, for I am not allowed to drink more than one glass a day, so that this store is quite enough for me. You write that you don't admit my being old. In that way you try to cover up your first present, so that people should not guess. But it is easy to discover that young people don't look through spectacles. I shall see you soon. The water is acting well, but it has become very tiresome here.

Altona, November 23, 1716

. . . Alexander Petrovitch writes that Petrushka has cut his fourth tooth; God grant he cut all so well, and that we may see him grow up, thus rewarding us for our former grief over his brothers. . . .

Spa, July 1, 1717

I yesterday received your letter of the 11th, in which you write of the illness [smallpox] of our daughters, and that the first, thank God! is getting better, while the other has taken to her bed, about which Alexander Danilovitch also writes me. But your changed style has made me very sad, as the bringer of this will tell you. For your letter was very differently written from usual. God grant we can hear the same about Anushka as about Lisenka. When you write for me to come quickly and that you are very lonesome, I believe you. The bringer of this will tell you how lonely I am without you, and I can say that, except those days when I was in Versailles and Marly, twelve days ago, I have had no great pleasure. But here I must stay some days, and when I finish drinking the water I will start that very day, for there are only seven hours by land and five days by water. God grant to see you in joy, which I wish from all my heart.

P.S.—I received this morning the glad news that Anushka is better, and therefore began to drink the water more joyously.

Spa, July 8, 1717

I congratulate you on this triumphal day of the Russian resurrection, only I am sorry that we celebrate it apart, as well as to-morrow's day of the Holy Apostles, the namesday of your old man and the brat. God grant that these days pass quickly, and that I can be with you sooner. The water, thank God, acts well, and I hope to finish the cure in a week from St. Peter's day. To-day I put on for the first time your camisole, and drank your health, but only very little, because it is forbidden.

P.S.—You write that you sent little because I drank little at the waters, which is true. I do not drink altogether more than five times a day, and spirit only once or twice, and not always, partly because it is strong, and partly because it is scarce. I think that it is very tiresome that we are so near and cannot see each other. God grant soon. On finishing this I drink once to your health.

Catherine to Peter

July 24, 1718

I and the children, thank God, are in good health. Although on my way to Petersburg Petrushka was a little weak with his last teeth, yet now with God's help he is quite well, and has cut three back teeth. I beg you, little father, for protection, for he has no little quarrel with me about you,—namely, because when I tell him that Papa has gone away he does not like it, but he likes it better and becomes glad when one says that Papa is here.

Reval, August 1, 1718

Thanks, my friend, for the figs, which came safely. I have had myself shorn here, and send you my shorn locks, though I know they will not be received.

Reval, July 1719

The new garden is very fine, and the trees on the seaside or the north very well planted, but on the south must be changed. Not one tree has been set out at the espalier, in which Neronof lied. They are now levelling the court which will be behind the house. All the earth-work is done in the garden. To tell the truth, it will be a marvel when finished. I send you some flowers and some of the mint which you yourself planted. Thank God, all is merry here, except that when one goes out to the villa, and you are not there, it is very lonesome.

July 1719

Thanks, my friend, for the present. 'Tis not dear to me because I planted it, but because it comes from thy hands. . . . Our only pleasure here is the garden. . . . The Frenchman, who made the new flower-beds, was walking one bad night and met Ivashka Khmelnitsky, and had such a bout with him [i.e., got drunk] that he was pushed off the bridge and sent to make flower-beds in the other world.

August 1719

The lion (Leo) sent by your Grace came to me. Quite wonderful, but he is not a lion, merely a playful cat from the dear Lion. He brought me a letter which pleased me, but kindly send me him whom I call Lion.

Reval, July 1723

The garden planted only two years ago has grown beyond belief, for the only big trees which you saw have in some places stretched their branches across the walk, and Aunty's tree, the stem of which was like a middle finger without the nail, has taken splendidly. The chestnuts all have fine crowns. The house is being plastered outside, but is ready within, and in one word we have hardly any where such a regular house. I send you some strawberries, which ripened before our arrival, as well as cherries. I am quite astonished that things are so early here, when it is in the same latitude as Petersburg.

Decree of Emperor Peter I for the Coronation of the Empress Catherine, May 1724

We, Peter I, Emperor and Autocrat of All Russia, etc., announce to all ecclesiastics, civil and military officers, and all others of the Russian nation, our faithful subjects, that there is no one who is not aware of the ever-present custom in Christian kingdoms by which emperors have their wives crowned, as well as examples of this same practice which has been employed many times by Emperors of the true Greek Faith. This includes the Emperor Basilides who had his wife Zenobia crowned, the Emperor Justinian and his wife Lupicine, the Emperor Heraclius and his wife Martine, the Emperor Leo the Philosopher and his wife Marie, and several others who have similarly placed the imperial crown on the heads of their wives, but whom we will not mention here because it would take too long.

It is also well known how greatly we have exposed our own person and faced the most serious dangers on behalf of our country during the course of the last twenty-one consecutive years of war; a war which, by the grace of God, we have concluded in such an honorable and an advantageous manner that Russia has never been able to boast a similar peace treaty nor ever formerly acquired such glory as brought to her by this war. The Empress Catherine, our very dear wife, has been a great assistance during all these dangers, not only in the forementioned war but also in some other expeditions upon which she voluntarily accompanied us and has helpfully counselled us as much as she was able in spite of the weaknesses of her sex, particularly at the battle against the Turks on the river Pruth when our army was reduced to 22,000 men and faced a Turkish army of 270,000 men. It was in this desperate situation that she displayed her praiseworthy zeal with a courage extraordinary in one of her sex, the report of which spread through the army and throughout the whole Empire. For these reasons, and by the power vested in us by God, we have resolved to

honor our wife with the imperial crown in recognition of all her suf-
ferings. This will be accomplished, please God, this winter at Moscow,
and we now announce this resolution to all our faithful subjects towards whom our imperial affection is unchanging.

4
Peter and His Correspondents

PETER AND MENSHIKOV[1]

Peter's closest friend was Alexander Menshikov, who had been recruited by the tsar into his "toy regiments" before 1689. Of unknown origins, Menshikov rose to be Governor of Saint Petersburg, a prince of the Holy Roman Empire, and the richest man in the empire. He was the first and foremost of the "fledglings," those people of obscure background who were raised above the old aristocracy by the will of the tsar.

May 19, 1705

I would long ago have been with you, except that for my sins and my misfortune I have been kept here in this way. On the very day I was starting from here, that is, Thursday the 15th, a fever took me and I was obliged to return. In the morning, after taking some medicine, I felt a little better. The next day I wished to go, but the fever returned stronger than before. The next day I felt better, and after that ill again. Thus we know that it is a tertian fever, on account of which I must stay here some time yet, hoping in the mercy of God Almighty that my illness will not be prolonged. Hey! how much I suffer from my illness, and also from grief that time is lost, as well as from my separation from you! But, for God's sake, do not be sad. I have written you all the details only that you should not receive them from others with exaggerations, as usual.

May 25, 1705

To my illness is added the grief of separation from you. I have endured it for a long time, but cannot stand it any more. Be good enough to come as soon as possible, so that I shall be merrier, as you yourself can judge. Bring with you an English doctor, and not many followers.

[1] Reprinted in Schuyler, *Peter the Great*, vol. 1, pp. 535–36; vol. 2, pp. 51–52.

April 1706

As you know, we are living here in paradise, but one idea never leaves me, about which you yourself know, but I place my confidence not on human will, but on the divine will and mercy.

May 10, 1706

Mein Bruder, it was with indescribable joy that I received the old man with letters when I was at Kronslot on the vice-admiral's ship "Elephant," and immediately, in thanks to God, we had a triple salute from the ships and the fort. God grant in joy to see you and the whole army again. And how glad, and then how noisy we were on account of it, the old man himself will tell. . . . For the good news that he brought us we gave him the rank of ensign, and I beg you to confirm it to him. To tell the truth, we were all glad to hear of these things, for, although we live in paradise, still we always had a pain in our hearts. Here, praise be to God, all is well, and there is nothing new of any sort. We shall start from here next month. Don't doubt about my coming. If God send no obstacle, I shall certainly start at the end of this month. Earlier than that it is impossible, alas! not because I am amusing myself, but the doctors have ordered me to keep still and take medicine for two weeks, after bleeding me, which they began yesterday. Immediately after that I shall come, for you yourself have seen in what state I was when we were separated from the army.

PETER AND THE PATRIARCH [2]

Peter wrote to the patriarch of the Orthodox church from Holland to explain his strange behavior of working in a shipyard as a common laborer.

September 20, 1697

We are in the Netherlands, in the town of Amsterdam, and by the mercy of God, and by your prayers, are alive and in good health, and, following the divine command given to our forefather Adam, we are hard at work. What we do is not from any need, but for the sake of learning navigation, so that, having mastered it thoroughly, we can, when we return, be victors over the enemies of Jesus Christ, and liberators of the Christians who live under them, which I shall not cease to wish for until my latest breath.

[2] Schuyler, *Peter the Great*, vol. 1, p. 358.

PETER TO ADMIRAL GOLOVIN [3]

Peter wrote to one of his naval commanders to express his anger over the Swedish defeat of the Saxon army of Augustus II of Poland.

June 1706

Herr Admiral: Before this I wrote to you of an unwished-for catastrophe, which I had heard from outsiders. Now, we have full information that all the Saxon army has been beaten by Rehnskjold, and has lost all its artillery. The treachery and cowardice of the Saxons are now plain—30,000 men beaten by 8,000! The cavalry, without firing a single round, ran away; more than half of the infantry, throwing down their muskets, disappeared, leaving our men alone, not half of whom, I think, are now alive. God knows what grief this news has brought us, and by giving money we have only bought ourselves misfortune. In this occurrence the treachery of Patkul will be plain, for I really think that he was taken prisoner only that no one might know about his treacherous conduct. The above-mentioned calamity, as well as the betrayal of the King by his own subjects, you can tell everybody (but put it much more mildly), for it cannot remain a secret. Still, tell it in detail to very few.

PETER TO APRAXIN [4]

Peter, in the first letter to the later commander of his navy, mourns the death of his mother. In the second letter he jokes about two of his older aides who were always reluctant to join him in his maneuvers.

February 7, 1694

I dumbly tell my misfortune and my last sorrow, about which neither my hand nor my heart can write in detail without remembering what the Apostle Paul says about not grieving for such things, and the verse of Esdras, "Call me again the day that is past." I forget all this as much as possible, as being above my reasoning and mind, for thus it has pleased the Almighty God, and all things are according to

---

[3] Reprinted in Schuyler, *Peter the Great,* vol. 2, p. 48.
[4] Reprinted in Schuyler, *Peter the Great,* vol. 1, pp. 283–84.

the will of their Creator. Amen! Therefore, like Noah, resting awhile from my grief, and leaving aside that which can never return, I write about the living.

February 9, 1694

Thy letter was handed to me by Michael Kuroyedof, and, after reflecting, I reported about it all to my Lord and Admiral, who, having heard my report, ordered me to write as follows. First: That the great lord is a man mighty bold for war, as well as on the watery way, as thou thyself knowest, and for that reason he does not wish to delay here longer than the last days of April. Second: That his Imperial brother, through love and even desire of this journey, like the Athenians seeking new things, has bound him to go, and does not wish to stay behind himself. Third: The rear-admiral will be Peter Ivanovitch Gordon. I think there will be nearly three hundred people of different ranks; and who, and what rank, and where, that I will write to thee presently. Hasten up with everything as quickly as you can, especially with the ship. Therefore I and my companions, who are working on the masts, send many respects. Keep well.

PETER TO THE KING OF DENMARK [5]

Peter wrote the Danish king in 1712 to blame him for the failure of a joint Russian-Danish expedition against Sweden.

March 1712

I think that your Majesty knows that I have not only furnished the number of troops agreed upon last year at Yaroslav with the King of Poland, but even three times as many, and besides that, for the common interests, I have come here myself, not sparing my health with the constant fatigue and long journey. But on my arrival here I find the army idle, because the artillery promised by you has not come, and when I asked your Vice-Admiral Segestet about it, he replied that it could not be given without your particular order. I am greatly at a loss to understand why these changes are made, and why favourable time is thus being wasted; from which, besides the loss in money and to the common interests, we shall gain nothing except the ridicule of our enemies. I have always been, and am, ready to help my allies in everything that the common interest demands. If you do not comply with this request of mine [to send the artillery], I can prove

⁵ Reprinted in Schuyler, *Peter the Great*, vol. 2, p. 282.

to you and the whole world that this campaign has not been lost by me, and I shall then not be to blame if, as I am inactive here, I am obliged to withdraw my troops, because on account of the dearness of things here it is a waste of money, and I cannot endure being dishonoured by the enemy.

PART TWO

PETER THE GREAT VIEWED BY HIS CONTEMPORARIES

5

The Official View

PROKOPOVICH: OUR MOSES, SOLOMON, AND DAVID [1]

Feofan Prokopovich (1861–1732), member of the hierarchy of the Russian Orthodox church and author of the Church Reform of 1721, was a close collaborator of the tsar and owed his rise to Peter's patronage. First a defector to Roman Catholicism and then a professor at the Kievan Academy after his return to Orthodoxy, he was discovered and rapidly promoted by Peter. Prokopovich was famous for his sermons on great occasions; he used his talents to justify the actions of his sovereign, and was one of the foremost exponents of absolute monarchy. The following sermon was delivered at Peter's funeral in 1725.

A FUNERAL ORATION FOR THE MOST ILLUSTRIOUS AND MOST SOVEREIGN EMPEROR AND AUTOCRAT OF ALL RUSSIA, PETER THE GREAT, FATHER OF THE FATHERLAND, DELIVERED IN THE CAPITAL CITY OF SAINT PETERSBURG, AT THE CHURCH OF THE FIRST APOSTLES, SAINTS PETER AND PAUL, BY THE RIGHT REVEREND THEOPHANOS, VICE-PRESIDENT OF THE MOST HOLY GOVERNING SYNOD, ARCHBISHOP OF PSKOV AND NARVA, ON THE 8TH DAY OF MARCH 1725.

What is this? O Russians, what have we lived to witness? What do we see? What are we doing? We are burying Peter the Great! Is it not

[1] Feofan Prokopovich, "Oration at the Funeral of Peter the Great," in Marc Raeff, ed., *Peter the Great: Reformer or Revolutionary?* (Boston: D. C. Heath and Company, 1963), pp. 76–78. Reprinted by permission of Marc Raeff.

a dream, an apparition? Alas, our sorrow is real, our misfortune certain! Contrary to everybody's wishes and hopes he has come to his life's end, he who has been the cause of our innumerable good fortunes and joys; who has raised Russia as if from among the dead and elevated her to such heights of power and glory; or better still, he who —like a true father of the fatherland—has given birth to Russia and nursed her. Such were his merits that all true sons of Russia wished him to be immortal; while his age and solid constitution gave everyone the expectation of seeing him alive for many more years; he has ended his life—O, horrible wound!—at a time when he was just beginning to live after many labors, troubles, sorrows, calamities, and perils of death. Do not we see well enough how much we have angered Thee, O Lord, and abused Thine patience! O, we are wretched and unworthy, our sins are immeasurable! He who does not see it is blind; he who sees it and does not confess his cruelty is obdurate. But why intensify our complaints and pity which we ought to assuage. How can we do it? For if we recall his great talents, deeds, and actions we shall feel the wound from the loss of such a great good, and we shall burst into tears. Alone a kind of lethargy or a death-like sleep can make us forget this truly great loss.

What manner of man did we lose? He was your Samson, Russia. No one in the world expected his appearance among you, and at his appearance the whole world marveled. He found but little strength in you, and on the model of his name he made your power strong like a rock and diamond. Finding an army that was disorderly at home, weak in the field, the butt of the enemy's derision, he created one that was useful to the fatherland, terrible to the enemy, renowned and glorious everywhere. In defending his fatherland he at the same time returned to it lands that had been wrested from it and augmented it by the acquisition of new provinces. Destroying those who had arisen against us, he at the same time broke and destroyed those who had evil designs on us; and closing the mouth of envy, he commanded the whole world to glorify him.

Russia, he was your first Japhet! He has accomplished a deed heretofore unheard of in Russia: the building and sailing of ships, of a new fleet that yields to none among the old ones. It was a deed beyond the whole world's expectation and admiration, and it opened up to thee, Russia, the way to all corners of the earth and carried thine power and glory to the remotest oceans, to the very limits set by thy own interests and by justice. Thine power which had been based on land he also has established on the sea, firmly and permanently.

He was your Moses, O Russia! For are not his laws like the strong visor of justice and the unbreakable fetters of crime! And do not his clear regulations illuminate your path, most high governing Senate, and that of all principal and particular administrations established by him! Are they not beacons of light in your search for what will be useful and what will avoid harm, for the security of the law-abiding and the detection of criminals? In truth, he has left us wondering wherein he has been best and most deserving of praise; was he loved and caressed more by good and honest men than hated by unrepentant sycophants and criminals?

O Russia, he was your Solomon, who received from the Lord reason and wisdom in great plenty. This is proven by the manifold philosophic disciplines introduced by him and by his showing and imparting to many of his subjects the knowledge of a variety of inventions and crafts unknown to us before his time. To this also bear witness the ranks and titles, the civil laws, the rules of social intercourse, propitious customs, and codes of behavior, and also the improvement of our external appearance. We see and marvel then at our fatherland; it has changed externally and internally, and it has become immeasurably better than it had been previously.

And he was your David and your Constantine, O Russian Church! The synodal administration is his work, and oral and written exhortations, too, have been his concern. The heart saved from the path of ignorance heaves a sigh of relief! What a zeal he has displayed in combatting superstition, adulatory hypocrisy, and the senseless, inimical, ruinous schism nesting in our midst. How great his desire and his endeavor to find the best pastoral talent, the truest divine wisdom, and the best improvement in everything.

Most distinguished man! Can a short oration encompass his immeasurable glory? Yet our present sad and pitiful state—moving us to tears and sighs—does not permit us to extend the discourse. Probably, in course of time, the thorns that butt our heart will dull, and then we shall speak of his deeds and virtues in fuller detail, even though we shall never be able to praise him adequately enough. But at this time, even remembering him but briefly, as if only touching the edges of his mantle, we see, my poor and unfortunate hearers, we see who has left us and whom we have lost.

Russians, it is not in vain that we feel exhausted by sadness and pity, not in vain, even though this great monarch, our father, has left us. He has gone—but he has not left us poor and wretched: his enormous power and glory—manifested in the deeds I spoke of before—have remained with us. As he has shaped his Russia, so she will remain: he has made her lovable to good men, and she will be loved; he has made her fearful to her enemies, and she will be feared; he has glorified her throughout the world, and her glory will not end. He has left us spiritual, civil, and military reforms. For if his perishable body has left us, his spirit remains.

Moreover, in departing forever he has not left us orphaned. How can we call ourselves orphans when we behold his sovereign successor, his true companion in life and the identically-minded ruler after his death, our most gracious and autocratic sovereign, great heroine and monarch, mother of all Russians! The world bears witness that the female sex is no hindrance to Your being like Peter the Great. Who does not know Your God-given, natural sovereign wisdom and maternal charity! And these two qualities have arisen and developed firmly, not merely because of Your cohabitation with such a ruler—for he cared little to have merely a companion for his bed—but by dint of Your sharing in his wisdom, labors, and misfortunes; so that over many years—like the gold refined in the crucible—he has formed an heir to his crown, power, and throne.

We can but expect that You will consolidate what he has done and complete what he has left unfinished, that You will preserve everything in good order! Courageous soul, only endeavor to overcome Your insufferable pain, a pain compounded by the loss of Your most beloved daughter; Yours is like a cruel wound that has been exacerbated by a new blow. And in this most bitter loss endeavor to be the way everybody has seen You alongside the active Peter, his companion in all labors and misfortunes.

And you, sons of Russia of all ranks and title, most noble estate, console your monarch and your mother by your loyalty and obedience; also console yourselves with the certain knowledge that in your monarch you see Peter's spirit—as if not all of Peter had withdrawn from you. For the rest, we bow before God our Lord who has thus visited us. Let merciful God, Father of all consolation, wipe the unquenchable tears of our sovereign Lady and her most beloved kin—daughters, grandchildren, nieces, and the whole imperial family; and let His merciful care sweeten the bitterness of their hearts and give us consolation. O Russia, seeing who and what manner of man has departed from you, behold also whom he has left to you. Amen.

LOMONOSOV: FATHER OF THE COUNTRY [2]

Michael Lomonosov (1711–65), most distinguished Russian historian, scientist, and literary figure of the eighteenth century, was the son of a peasant from Archangel Province. He was raised in the Petrine era and benefitted from the new thrusts of the age to emerge as one of the primary figures of the European

[2] M. V. Lomonosov, "Panegyric to the Sovereign Emperor, Peter the Great," trans. Ronald Hingley, in Marc Raeff, ed., *Russian Intellectual History: An Anthology* (Harcourt, Brace & World, Inc., 1966), pp. 42–48. Reprinted by permission of the publisher.

Enlightenment. Lomonosov, therefore, considered Peter the Great to be one of Russia's greatest heroes. In the following oration written for the coronation of Peter's daughter, in addition to the normal dosage of eighteenth-century rhetoric, there is a strong measure of honest feeling which gave substance to the emerging Petrine myth.

Exemplary on land, peerless on the waters in His might and military glory was our Great Defender!

From this brief account, which contains but a small part of His labors, I already feel fatigue, O my Listeners; yet I see the great and far-reaching field of His merits before me! And so that my strength and limited time may suffice to complete the drift of my discourse, I shall make all possible haste.

For the foundation and bringing into action of so great a naval and land force, and also for the construction of new towns, fortresses, and harbors, for the joining of rivers with great canals, for the strengthening of frontiers with ramparts, for long-lasting war, for frequent and distant campaigns, for the construction of public and private buildings in a new architectural style, for the finding of experienced persons and all other means for the dissemination of science and the arts, for the maintenance of new court and state officials—how vast a treasury was needed for these things anyone can easily imagine, and conclude that the revenues of Peter's Forefathers could not suffice for this. Wherefore the sagacious Sovereign did strive most earnestly to increase internal and external state revenues without ruining the people. And He had the native wit to perceive that by means of a single institution not only would great gains accrue to the treasury, but the general tranquillity and safety of His subjects would also be assured. For at a time when the total number of the Russian people and the place of residence of each person were not yet known, there was no curb on arbitrary conduct, and no one was forbidden to change his place of residence or to wander about as the whim took him. The streets were filled with shameless, loafing beggars; the roads and great rivers were often blocked by the thieves and by whole regiments of murderous brigands who brought ruin to towns and villages alike. The wise Hero converted harm into benefit, laziness into industriousness, pillagers into defenders; when He had counted the multitude of His subjects, He bound each one to his dwelling and imposed a light, but fixed, tax; in this way the internal revenues of the treasury were increased, and a definite amount of such revenue was assured—and, likewise, the number of persons on recruiting lists. Industriousness and strict military training were also increased. Many who, under previous conditions, would have been dangerous robbers He compelled to be ready to die for their country.

I say nothing of the assistance afforded in this matter by other wise institutions, but will mention the increase of external revenues. Divine Providence aided the good designs and efforts of Peter, through His hand opening new ports on the Varangian [Baltic] Sea at towns conquered by His valor and erected by His own labors. Great rivers were joined for the more convenient passage of Russian merchants, duty regulations were established, and commercial treaties with various peoples were concluded. What benefit proceeded from the growth of this abundance within and without has been clear from the very foundation of these institutions, for while continuing to fight a burdensome war for twenty years Russia was free from debts.

What, then, have all Peter's great deeds already been depicted in my feeble sketch? Oh, how much labor still remains for my thoughts, voice, and tongue! I ask you, my Listeners, out of your knowledge to consider how much assiduous effort was required for the foundation and establishment of a judiciary, and for the institution of the Governing Senate, the Most Holy Synod, the state colleges, the chancelleries, and the other governmental offices with their laws, regulations, and statutes; for the establishment of the table of ranks and the introduction of decorations as outward tokens of merit and favor; and, finally, for foreign policy, missions, and alliances with foreign powers. You may contemplate all these things yourselves with minds enlightened by Peter. It remains to me only to offer a brief sketch of it all. Let us suppose that before the beginning of Peter's enterprises someone had happened to leave his native Russia for distant lands where His name had not thundered forth—if such a land there be on this earth. Returning later to Russia, he would see new knowledge and arts among the people, new dress and customs, new architecture and household furnishings, newly built fortresses, a new fleet, and a new army; he would see not only the different aspects of all these things but also a change in the courses of rivers and in the boundaries of the seas. What would he then think? He could come to no other conclusion than that he had been on his travels for many centuries, or that all this had been achieved in so short a time by the common efforts of the whole human race or by the creative hand of the Almighty, or, finally, that it was all a vision seen in a dream.

From these words of mine, which reveal scarcely more than the mere shadow of Peter's glorious deeds, it may be seen how great they are! But what is one to say of the terrible and dangerous obstacles encountered on the path of His mighty course? They have exalted His honor the more! The human condition is subject to such changes that undesirable consequences arise from favorable origins, and desirable consequences from unfavorable origins. What could have been more unpropitious to our prosperity than that, while He was engaged in reforming Russia, Peter and the country were threatened by attacks from without, by afflictions from within, and by dangers on all sides, and dire consequences were brewing? The war hampered domestic affairs, and domestic affairs hampered the war, which worked injury even before it had started. The Great Sovereign set out from His native land with a great embassy to see the states of Europe and to acquire knowledge of their advantages, so that on His return He might use them for the benefit of His subjects. Hardly had He crossed the frontiers of His dominion than He everywhere encountered great obstacles which had been set up secretly. However, I do not mention them now, since they are known to all the world. It seems to me that even inanimate objects sensed the oncoming danger to Russia's hopes. The waters of the Divina sensed it and opened a path for their future Master amid the thick ice to save Him from the cunning snares that had been laid. Pouring forth, they proclaimed to the shores of the Baltic the dangers which He had overcome. Having escaped from danger, He hurried on his joyous path, finding pleasure for His eyes and heart and enriching His mind. But alas! He unwillingly cut short His glorious course. What conflict He suffered within Himself! On the one hand was the pull of curiosity and of knowledge needful to the homeland; on the other hand there was the homeland itself, which had fallen on evil days and which, holding forth its hands to Him as to its only hope, exclaimed: "Return, return quickly; I am rent within by traitors! Thou art traveling in the interests of my happiness; I recognize this with gratitude, but do Thou first tame those who are raging. Thou hast parted from Thy household and with Thy dear ones to increase my glory; I acknowledge it eagerly, but do Thou allay the dangerous disorder. Thou hast left behind the crown and scepter given to Thee by God and hidest the rays of Thy Majesty behind a humble appearance for the sake of my enlightenment; with joyous hope do I desire it, but do Thou ward off the dark storm of turbulence from the domestic horizon." Affected by such feelings, He returned to calm the terrible tempest. Such hindrances impeded our Hero in His glorious exploits! How many enemies surrounded Him on all sides! From abroad war was made by Sweden, Poland, the Crimea, Persia, many eastern nations, and the Ottoman Porte; at home there were the strel'tsy, the dissenters, the Cossacks, and the brigands. In His own household villainies, hatred, and acts of treachery against His most precious life were fomented by His own blood. To describe all in detail would be difficult, and it would be painful to hear! Let us return to the joy of a joyous era. The Almighty helped Peter to overcome all grievous obstacles and to exalt Russia, fostering His piety, sagacity, magnanimity, courage, sense of justice, forbearance, and industriousness. His zeal and faith in God in all His enterprises are well known. His first joy was the Lord's house. He was not just a worshiper attending divine service, but Himself the chief officiant. He heightened the attention and devotion of the worshipers with His monarchic voice; and He would stand somewhere away from the sovereign's place, by the side of ordinary choristers, before God. We have many examples of His piety, but one shall now suffice. Going out to meet the body of the holy and brave Prince Alexander, He moved the whole city and moved the waters of the Neva with an act full of devotion. Wondrous spectacle! At the oars were the Bearers of various Orders, while in the stern the Monarch Himself was steering and, before all the people, lifting His anointed hands to the labor of simple men in the name of His faith. Made strong by His faith, He escaped the frequent assault of bloodthirsty traitors. On the day of the battle of Poltava the Lord shielded His head with power from on high and did not permit the death-dealing metal to touch it! As the Lord had once crumbled the wall of Jericho, He crumbled before Peter the wall of Narva—not while blows were being struck from fire-breathing engines, but during divine service.

Sanctified and protected by piety, He was endowed by God with peerless wisdom. What seriousness in counsel, unfeigned brevity of speech, precision of images, dignity of utterance, thirst for learning, diligent attention to prudent and useful discourses, and what unwavering intelligence [showed] in the eyes and entire countenance! Through these gifts of Peter, Russia took on a new appearance, foundation was laid for the arts and sciences, missions and alliances were instituted, the cunning designs of certain powers against our country were thwarted, while among Sovereigns some had their kingdoms and autocratic rights preserved, and to others the crown wrested from them by their foes was restored. Complementing the wisdom lavished on Him from on high and clearly manifested in everything which has been said above was His heroic courage; with the former He astounded the universe, with the latter He struck fear into His enemies. In His most tender childhood He showed fearlessness in military exercises. When all the observers of a new enterprise—the throwing of grenades on to a designated place—were exceedingly fearful of injury, the young Sovereign strove with all His might to watch from nearby, and was scarcely restrained by the tears of His Mother, the pleas of His Brother, and the supplications of dignitaries. On His travels in foreign states in pursuit of learning, how many dangers He scorned for the sake of Russia's renewal! Sailing over the inconstant depths of the sea served him for entertainment. How many times the waves of

the sea, raising their proud crests, were witnesses of unblenching daring as, cleft by the swift-running fleet, they struck the ships and combined with raging flame and metal roaring through the air into a
single danger, but failed to terrify Him! Who can without terror picture Peter flying over the fields of Poltava amidst His army, drawn up
for battle, a hail of enemy bullets whistling around His head, His
voice raised aloft through the tumult urging His regiments to fight
bravely. Nor couldst thou, sultry Persia, halt our Hero's onset with
thy swift rivers, miry swamps, high mountain precipices, poisonous
springs, burning sands, or sudden raids of turbulent peoples, as thou
couldst not stop His triumphal entry into cities filled with hidden
weapons and guile.

For the sake of brevity I offer no more examples of His heroic spirit,
O my Hearers, and I make no mention of the many battles and victories that occurred in His presence and under His leadership; but I
do speak of His generosity, the generosity characteristic of great
Heroes, which adorns victories and moves the human heart more than
bold deeds. In victories the courage of the soldiers, the help of allies,
and the opportuneness of place and time have a share, and chance ap-
propriates the greatest share, as if taking what belongs to it. But everything belongs to the conqueror's generosity alone. He wins the most
glorious victory who can conquer himself. In [this victory] neither soldiers, nor allies, nor time, nor place, nor yet that chance itself which
rules over human affairs have even the slightest portion. True, reason admires the victor, but it is the heart which loves the man of
generous spirit. Such was our Great Defender. He would lay down
His wrath together with His weapons, and not only were none of His
enemies deprived of their lives merely because they had borne arms
against Him, but they were even shown honor beyond compare. Tell
me, you Swedish generals who were captured at Poltava, what did you
think when, expecting to be bound, you were girt with your own
swords which you had raised against us; when, expecting to be put
into dungeons, you were put to sit at the Victor's table; when, expecting mockery, you were hailed as our teachers. What a generous Conqueror you had!

Justice is akin to generosity and is often linked with it. The
first duty of rulers set over nations by God is to govern the realm in
righteousness and truth, to reward merit and punish crime. Although
military matters and other great concerns and, in particular, His premature death much hindered the Great Sovereign in establishing im-
mutable and clear laws for everything, yet how much labor He expended in this matter is testified beyond doubt by the many decrees,
statutes, and regulations, the drafting of which deprived Him of many
days of relaxation and many nights of sleep. God has willed that a

Daughter like unto so great a Sire should complete these things and bring them to perfection during Her untroubled and blessed rule.

But though justice was not established to perfection in clear and systematic laws, yet was justice inscribed in His heart. Though not everything was written in books, it was carried out in fact. At the same time mercy was favored in the courtroom in those very instances when villainies which had hindered many of His deeds seemed to compel severity. Of many examples, one will serve. Having forgiven many distinguished persons their grievous crimes, He proclaimed His heartfelt joy by taking them to His table and by firing cannon. [However,] He is not made despondent by the execution of the strel'tsy. Imagine to yourselves and reflect on what zeal for justice, pity for His subjects, and His own danger were saying in His heart. Innocent blood has been shed in the houses and streets of Moscow, widows are weeping, orphans are sobbing, violated women and girls are moaning, my relatives were put to death in my house before my eyes, and a sharp weapon was held against my heart. I was preserved by God, I endured these things, eluded danger, and took my way outside the city. Now they have cut short my beneficial journey, openly taking up arms against the homeland. If I do not take revenge for all this, averting eventual doom by means of execution, I foresee town squares filled with corpses, plundered houses, wrecked churches, Moscow beset by flames on all sides, and my beloved country plunged into smoke and ashes. For all these disasters, tears, and bloodshed God will hold me answerable. Mindful of this ultimate judgment, He was compelled to resort to severity.

Nothing can serve me so well to demonstrate the kindness and gentleness of His heart as His incomparable graciousness toward His subjects. Superbly endowed as He was, elevated in His Majesty, and exalted by most glorious deeds, He did but the more increase and adorn these things by His incomparable graciousness. Often He moved amongst His subjects simply, countenancing neither the pomp that proclaims the monarch's presence nor servility. Often anyone afoot was free to meet Him, to follow Him, to walk along with Him, to start a conversation if so inclined. In former times many Sovereigns were carried on the shoulders and heads of their slaves; graciousness exalted Him above these very Sovereigns. At the very time of festivity and relaxation important business would be brought to Him; but the importance did not decrease gaiety, nor did simplicity lessen the importance. How He awaited, received, and greeted His loyal subjects! What gaiety there was at His table! He asked questions, listened, answered, discussed as with friends; and whatever time was saved at table by the small number of dishes was spent in gracious conversation. Amid so many cares of state He lived at ease as among friends. Into how many tiny huts of craftsmen did He bring His Majesty, and heartened with His presence His most lowly, but skilled and loyal, servants. How often He joined them in the exercise of their crafts and in various labors. For He attracted more by example than He compelled by force. And if there was anything which then seemed to be compulsion, it now stands revealed as a benefaction. His idea of relaxation was to change His labors. Not only day or morning but even the sun at its rising shone upon Him in many places as He was engaged in various labors. The business of the governmental, administrative, and judicial offices instituted by Him was carried on in His presence. The various crafts made speedy progress not only through His supervision but also through the assistance of His hands; public buildings, ships, harbors, fortresses ever beheld Him, having Him as guide in their foundation, supporter in their labor, and rewarder on completion. What of His travels or, rather, swift-soaring flights? Hardly had the White Sea heard the voice of His command before it was already felt by the Baltic; scarcely had His ships' wake disappeared on the waters of the Sea of Azov before the thundering Caspian waves were making way for Him. And you great rivers, the Southern Divina and the Northern Divina, Dnieper, Don, Volga, Bug, Vistula, Oder, Elbe, Danube, Seine, Thames, Rhine, and others, tell me, how often were you granted the honor of reflecting the image of Peter the Great in your waters? Will you tell me? I cannot count them! Now we can only contemplate with joyous amazement the roads along which He went, the tree under which He rested, the spring that quenched His thirst, the places where He labored with humble persons as a humble workman, where He wrote laws, where He made plans of boats, harbors, and fortresses, and where at the same time He conversed with His subjects as a friend. In His care and labors for us He was in constant motion, like the stars of the sky in their course, like the ebb and flow of the tide.

In the midst of fire in the battlefield, amid weighty government deliberations, amid the diverse machinery of various crafts, amid a numberless multitude of peoples engaged in the building of towns, harbors, and canals, amid the roaring breakers of the White, Black, Baltic, and Caspian seas and of the very Ocean itself—wherever I turn in spirit, everywhere do I behold Peter the Great in sweat, in dust, in smoke, in flame; and I cannot convince myself that it is not many Peters everywhere, but a single one, not a thousand years, but one short life. With whom shall I compare the Great Sovereign? In both ancient and modern times I behold Rulers termed great. And in truth they are great when compared with others; but compared with Peter they are little. One has conquered many states but has left his own country untended. Another has vanquished a foe who was already called great, but has spilled the blood of his citizens on all sides solely to gratify his own ambition and instead of a triumphal return has heard the weeping and lamentation of his country. Some were adorned with many virtues but, instead of lifting up their country, were unable to keep it from sinking. Some have been warriors on land but have feared the sea. Some have ruled the waves but feared to put in to shore. Some have loved learning but feared the drawn sword. Some have feared neither steel nor water nor fire, but have lacked understanding of man's estate and heritage. I shall quote no examples except that of Rome. But even Rome falls short. What was achieved in the two hundred and fifty years from the First Punic War to Augustus by Nepos, Scipio, Marcellus, Regulus, Metellus, Cato, and Sulla—as much was achieved by Peter in the short period of His life. Then to whom shall I liken our Hero? I have often pondered the nature of Him whose all-powerful hand rules sky, land, and sea. Let His breath blow and the waters shall pour forth; let Him touch the mountains and they shall be lifted up. But a limit has been set to human thoughts! They cannot grasp the Deity! He is usually pictured in human form. And so, if a man must be found who, in our conception, resembles God, I find none excepting Peter the Great.

For His great services to the country He has been called Father of the Country. But the title is too small for Him. Say, what name shall we give Him in return for begetting His Daughter, our most gracious Sovereign, who has ascended Her Father's throne in courage, vanquished proud enemies, pacified Europe, and lavished Her benefactions on Her subjects?

Hear us, O God, and reward us, O Lord! For Peter's great labors, for the solicitude of Catherine, for the tears and sighs that the two Sisters, Peter's two Daughters, poured forth when taking Their farewell, for all Their incomparable benefactions to Russia, reward us with length of days and with Posterity.

And Thou, Great Soul, shining in eternity and casting Heroes into obscurity with Thy brilliance, do Thou exult. Thy Daughter reigns; Thy Grandson is heir; a Great-grandson has been born in accordance with our desire; we have been exalted, strengthened, enlightened, and adorned by Thee; by Her we have been delivered, enheartened, defended, enriched, glorified. Accept as a sign of gratitude this unworthy offering. Thy merits are greater than all our efforts.

6

The View from Inside the Empire

KORB: TORTURES MOST ATROCIOUS [1]

*Baron Johan G. Korb was secretary of the Austrian lega-
tion at Peter's court, and kept a Latin diary which was published in Austria during Peter's lifetime and caused substantial
friction between the two governments. Korb's account of Peter's
punishment of the rebellious streltsy (palace guards) in 1699 presented an unflattering picture of the vengeful tsar to western
eyes.*

September 5, 1698

The report of the Czar's arrival had spread through the city. The
Boyars and principal Muscovites flocked in numbers at an early hour
to the place where it became known he had spent the night, to pay
their court. Great was the crowd of congratulators, who came to prove
by the promptitude of their obsequiousness the constancy of their
loyalty to their sovereign. Although the chief ambassador, Francis,
son of James Lefort, would receive nobody that day, alleging the fatigue occasioned by such long and uninterrupted travelling, nevertheless his Majesty the Czar received all that came, with an alacrity that
showed as if he wished to be beforehand with his subjects in eagerness.
Those who, according to the fashion of that country, would cast themselves upon the ground to worship majesty, he lifted up graciously
from their groveling posture, and embraced with a kiss, such as is only
due among private friends. If the razor, that plied promiscuously
among the beards of those present, can be forgiven the injury it did,
the Muscovites may truly reckon that day among the happiest of their
lives. Knes Alexis Simonowicz Schachin, General-in-Chief of the Czar's
troops, was the first who submitted the encumbrance of his long
beard to the razor.

[1] Baron Korb, *Scenes from the Court of Peter the Great*, ed. F. L. Glaser (New
York: Nicholas L. Brown, 1921), pp. 31–32, 38–40, 61–66, 71–72.

Nor can they consider it any disgrace, as their sovereign is the first to show the example—their sovereign to whose wish or command they deem it a holy and religious command to devote their lives. Nor was there anybody left to laugh at the rest. They were all born to the same fate. Nothing but superstitious awe for his office exempted the Patriarch. Prince Lehugowicz Tzerkasky was let off out of reverence for his advanced years, and Tichon Nikitowicz Stresnow out of honor due to one who had been guardian of the Czarine. All the rest had to conform to the guise of foreign nations, and the razor eliminated the ancient fashion.

September 14, 1698

. . . Dinner was not yet over when his Majesty left the room in a rage with his General-in-Chief, Schachin, with whom he had been warmly disputing; and nobody knew what he was going to do. It was known later that he had gone to question the soldiers, to learn from them how many colonels and other regimental officers that general-in-chief had made without reference to merit, merely for money. In a short time when he came back, his wrath had grown to such a pitch that he drew his sword, and facing the general-in-chief, horrified his guests with this threat: "By striking thus, I will mar thy mal-government."

Boiling over with well-grounded anger, he appealed to Prince Romadonowski, and Dumnoi Mikitim Mosciwicz; but finding them excuse the general-in-chief, he grew so hot that he startled all the guests by striking right and left, he knew not where, with his drawn sword. Knes Romadonowski had to complain of a cut finger, and another of a slight wound on the head. Mikitim Mosciwicz was hurt in the hand as the sword was returning from a stroke. A blow far more deadly was aiming at the general-in-chief, who beyond a doubt would have been stretched in his gore by the Czar's right hand, had not General Lefort (who was almost the only one who might have ventured it), catching the Czar in his arms, drawn back his hand from the stroke. But the Czar, taking it ill that any person should dare to hinder him from sating his just wrath, wheeled around upon the spot, and struck his unwelcome impeder a hard blow on the back. . . . Merriment followed this dire tempest: the Czar, with a face full of smiles, was present at the dancing . . . and the hilarity of the fete was protracted till half-past five in the morning.

First Execution, October 10, 1698

To this exhibition of avenging justice the Czar's Majesty invited all the ambassadors of foreign sovereigns, as it were to assert anew on his return that sovereign prerogative of life and death which the rebels had disputed with him. . . . A German major was then my companion; he concealed his nationality in a Muscovite dress, besides which he relied upon his military rank and the liberty he might take in consequence of being entitled by reason of his being in the service of the Czar to share in the privileges of the Muscovites. He mingled with the thronging crowd of Muscovites, and when he came back announced that five rebel heads had been cut off in that spot by an ax that had been swung by the noblest arm of all Muscovy. . . . On the opposite side of the stream there were a hundred criminals set upon those little Muscovite carts which the natives call Sboesk, awaiting the hour of the death they had to undergo. . . . Then the proclamation of the sentence began, the Czar exhorting all the bystanders to mark well its tenor. As the executioner was unable to dispatch so many criminals, some military officers, by command of the Czar, came under compulsion to aid in the butcher's task. The guilty were neither chained nor fettered; but logs were tied to their legs, which hindered them from walking fast, but still allowed them the use of their feet. They strove of their own accord to ascend the ladder, making the sign of the cross towards the four quarters of the world; they themselves covered their eyes and faces with a piece of linen (which is a national custom); very many putting their necks into the halter sprang headlong of themselves from the gallows, in order to precipitate their end. There were counted 230 that expiated their flagitious conduct by halter and gibbet.

Second Execution, October 13, 1698

Although all those that were accomplices of the rebellion were condemned to death, yet the Czar's majesty would not dispense with strict investigation. The more so since the unripe years of judgement of many seemed to bespeak mercy, as they were, as one may say, rather victims of error than of deliberate crime. In such case the penalty of death was commuted into some corporal infliction—such as, for instance, the cutting off their ears and noses, to mark them with ignominy for life—a life to be passed, not as previously, in the heart of the realm, but in various and barbarous place on the frontiers of Muscovy. To such places fifty were transported today, after being castigated in the manner prescribed.

Third Execution, October 17, 1698

It was reported by a number of persons that today again the Czar had himself executed public vengeance upon some traitors.

The tortures—most atrocious—to which Lieutenant Colonel Kolpakow has been continually subjected for some time, so rent his flesh that he lost the power both of speech and motion. In consequence he was earnestly commended to the skill and attention of the Czar's physician. Through negligence the doctor had left a knife in his cell, with which he had probably been preparing medicaments. Kolpakow . . . drew the knife across his throat, hoping to find death by cutting that channel of life; but when his hand had nearly accomplished the deed, his strength failed him, and he was cured of his wound, and today was dragged back again to the torture.

October 27, 1698

The two bedchamberwomen named above were buried alive, if we are to believe what rumor has bruited abroad. . . . Prince Romadonowski, who was chief of four regiments of strelitz before their revolt, laid four strelitz low with the same weapon.—His Majesty urging him to it. The more cruel Alexasca went boasting of twenty heads that he had chopped off. . . . Three hundred and thirty that were all led out together to the ax's fatal stroke impurpled the plain far and wide with civil—'tis true—but impious blood. . . . The Czar himself, sitting in his saddle, looked on with dry eyes at the whole tragedy—at this frightful butchery of a multitude of men—being only irate that several of the Boyars had performed this unaccustomed function with trembling hands—*for that no fatter victim could be immolated to God than a wicked man.*

KAMPFER: GREAT BEAUTY AND LIVELY MANNER [3]

A German traveler, Englebert Kampfer, visited Moscow in 1683 while on a trip to Astrakhan. In a temporary post as secretary to the Swedish envoy, he was given an audience with Peter and his half brother Ivan who were serving as co-tsars.

Here we got off our horses, and, handing our swords to a servant, walked up some steps and passed through a building magnificent with gilded vaults, and then through an open stone passage, again to the left, and through an ante-room in the audience hall, the floor of which was covered with Turkish carpets, where we came to the "piercing eyes" of their Tsarish Majesties. Both their Majesties sat, not in

[3] From Kampfer's manuscript diary, reprinted in Schuyler, *Peter the Great*, vol. 2, pp. 125–27.

the middle, but somewhat to the right side of the hall, next to the middle column, and sat on a silver throne like a bishop's chair, somewhat raised and covered with red cloth, as was most of the hall. Over the throne hung a holy picture. The Tsars wore, over their coats, robes of silver cloth woven with red and white flowers, and, instead of sceptres, had long golden staves bent at the end like bishops' croziers, on which, as on the breastplate of their robes, their breasts and their caps, glittered white, green and other precious stones. The elder drew his cap down over his eyes several times and, with looks cast down on the floor, sat almost immovable. The younger had a frank and open face, and his young blood rose to his cheeks as often as anyone spoke to him. He constantly looked about, and his great beauty and his lively manner—which sometimes brought the Muscovite magnates into confusion—struck all of us so much that had he been an ordinary youth and no imperial personage we would gladly have laughed and talked with him. The elder was seventeen, and the younger sixteen years old. When the Swedish Envoy gave his letters of credence, both Tsars rose from their places, slightly bared their heads and asked about the king's health, but Ivan, the elder, somewhat hindered the proceedings through not understanding what was going on, and gave his hand to be kissed at the wrong time. Peter was so eager that he did not give the secretaries the usual time for raising him and his brother from their seats and touching their heads: he jumped up at once, put his own hand to his hat and began quickly to ask the usual question: "Is his royal Majesty, Carolus of Sweden, in good health?" He had to be pulled back until the elder brother had a chance of speaking.

WEBER: SO MUCH WINE AND VODKA [4]

Friedrich Weber was the Dutch envoy in Russia until 1720 and left behind two volumes of memoirs on his experiences.

The Tsar went to Cronslot, where we also followed in a galley, but in consequence of a great storm we were obliged to remain at anchor in this open boat for two days and two nights, without lights, without beds, without food and drink. When at last we arrived at Cronslot, the Tsar invited us to his villa at Peterhof. We went with a fair wind, and at dinner warmed ourselves to such a degree with old Hungarian wine, although His Majesty spared himself, that on rising from the table we could scarcely keep on our legs, and when we had

[4] Friedrich Christian Weber, *The Present State of Russia* (London, 1723), pp. 107–9.

been obliged to drain quite a quart apiece from the hands of the
Tsaritsa we lost all our senses, and in that condition they carried us
out to different places, some to the garden, some to the woods, while
the rest lay on the ground here and there. At four o'clock they woke
us up and again invited us to the summer-house, where the Tsar gave
us each an axe and bade us follow him. He led us into a young wood
where he pointed out trees which it was necessary to fell in order to
make an alley straight to the sea, about a hundred paces long, and told
us to cut down the trees. He himself began work on the spot (there
were seven of us besides the Tsar), and although this unaccustomed
work, especially in our far from sober condition, was not at all to our
liking, we nevertheless cut boldly and diligently, so that in about three
hours the alley was ready and the fumes of wine had entirely evap-
orated. None of us did himself any harm except Minister X, who
unconsciously cut one tree and was knocked down by another, badly
scratched. After verbal thanks we received our real recompense after
supper in a second drink, which was so strong that we were taken
to our beds unconscious. We had hardly succeeded in sleeping an hour
or two before the Tsar's favourite appeared, pulled us out of our beds,
and dragged us against our will to the room of a Circassian prince,
asleep there with his wife, where before his bed we had again to drink
so much wine and vodka that on the following day none of us could
remember who brought us home. At eight o'clock in the morning we
were invited to the palace to breakfast, which consisted of a good
glass of vodka, and afterwards were taken to the foot of a little hill and
made to mount some wretched country nags without saddles or stir-
rups, and ride about for an hour in sight of their Majesties, who stood
at the window. At dinner again for the fourth time we had to drink
freely. As the wind was strong we were put into the Tsar's covered
boat, in which the Tsaritsa with her maid of honour had occupied
the cabin, while the Tsar stood with us on the open deck and assured
us that in spite of the strong wind ahead we should arrive at Cronstadt
at four o'clock. But after we had manoeuvred about for two hours we
were caught by such a frightful squall, that the Tsar, leaving all his
jokes, himself took hold of the rudder, and in that danger displayed
not only great knowledge of manoeuvring, but unusual physical
strength and steadfastness. The Tsaritsa, in consequence of the waves
which beat over the whole boat, and the dripping rain which ran into
her cabin, was sheltered under some benches which were tilted up for
the purpose, and in that difficult position showed also great presence
of mind. We all gave ourselves up wholly to the will of God, and con-
soled ourselves with the thought that we should drown in company
with such exalted personages. All effects of the drink disappeared very
quickly, and we were filled with thoughts of repentance. Four boyers

on which were the Court of the Tsaritsa and our servants, were tossed about by the waves and driven ashore. Our boat, on account of its great strength and the experienced sailors, after seven dangerous hours reached the harbour of Cronstadt, where the Tsar left us, saying: "A pleasant night. The amusement was rather too strong." The next day he had an attack of fever. As the rain had drenched us for the whole day, and besides that we had sat for four hours up to our waist in water, we lighted a fire on the island, and not having with us any clothes or beds or any of our other things, which were with our servants, we stripped, wrapped ourselves in rough coverings which we borrowed from the peasants, and during the night as we warmed ourselves at the fire had time enough to express our ideas on the wretchedness and uncertainties of human life. After this excursion we all fell ill with fevers or some other malady.

BERGHOLZ: A COURT OF FAVORITES [5]

Bergholz, an aide-de-camp of the duke of Holstein, visited the court of Saint Petersburg in 1721.

The Court of the Tsar is very mean, for he has almost no one in his service but a few orderlies, some of whom are indeed of good family, but most of low birth. These young men, his greatest favourites, enjoy however, no little influence with him. There are in all three or four to whom he holds much. One is the nephew of General Buturlin; the second, Tchevkin, is so like his twin-brother that they can only be distinguished by their clothes. They say that when the Tsar went to Danzig, he took them with him only on account of their great resemblance to each other. The one who was least able to suit himself to his humour he gave over to the Tsarina. The third favourite and orderly is named Tatistchef, and is of a Russian family. The fourth and last, Basil, was a poor young fellow in the Tsar's choir, and as the Tsar himself is a singer, and every Sunday and feast-day stands in the same row with the common choristers and sings with them in church, he took such a great liking to him that he can scarcely live an instant without him. These two last are his greatest favourites, since generally when the Tsar is alone or in a small company he eats at the same table with them. I am of opinion that the Tsar cares still more for Basil, since he seizes him by the head perhaps a hundred times a day and kisses him, and even lets the highest Ministers stand and wait

[5] Reprinted in Schuyler, *Peter the Great,* vol. 1, pp. 546–47.

while he goes and talks to him. This man is of poor common people, and has never had any other education than that of a chorister. Besides, his appearance is quite common and ordinary. In a word, he is, according to all appearance, a simple inoffensive youth, and yet the finest people of the whole realm pay their court to him.

MÜNNICH: A GENIUS OF THE FIRST QUALITY [6]

Marshal de Münnich was brought into Russia by Tsar Peter to take up the construction of the canal system which the tsar had planned and which was going badly. Münnich remained in Russia and enjoyed an extremely active military and political career.

The emperor was always in the Senate, often twice a day and long into the night. There was not one College which he did not visit with astonishing dedication. Never has there been a prince who has worked harder or maintained such constant interest in the welfare of his people. A genius of the first quality, he would promptly and precisely decide matters which obstructed the work of the Senators and the Colleges, scratching his feelings and wishes on a scrap of paper in a few words. Never was there a conqueror with a more definite point of view or with more confidence about the certainty of his conquests than Peter the Great; he even employed vast sums of money to build the cities and the fortresses of Petersburg and Kronstadt and other ports on Swedish territories long before he was assured of the conditions of a peace treaty which then seemed very doubtful and very distant. The many facets of his genius multiplied themselves to meet multiplying obstacles. His actions amazed all of his neighbors and gave him a superiority over them, so much so that all of Europe in a common voice gave this incomparable prince the name of Great.

THE OLD-BELIEVERS: "THE ANTICHRIST" [7]

The followers of the "old belief," called raskolniki or schismatics, emerged from the church crisis of the seventeenth century and were deeply attached to Muscovite traditions and Orthodox ritual. They had left the body of the official church and formed

[6] Marshal de Münnich, *Ébauche pour donner une idée de la forme du gouvernement de l'empire Russe* (Copenhagen, 1774), pp. 31–32; trans. L. J. Oliva.

[7] Reprinted in Schuyler, *Peter the Great*, vol. 2, pp. 193–94.

*a large part of the Russian population in Peter's time. They
viewed Peter's reforms as Satan's final assault on the True Faith,
and their feelings provide a good antidote to the prevailing western view of Peter as progressive and enlightened. The following
is an apocalyptic tract found in the Solovietsky Monastery.*

The Apostle says first comes a falling away, then is revealed the
man of sin, the son of perdition, the Anti-Christ. First came the falling away from the holy faith by the Tsar Alexis in the year 666 [1666-
ED.], the number of the beast thus fulfilling the prophecy. And after
him there reigned on the throne his first-born son Peter, from his
second and unlawful marriage. He was consecrated to the throne of
all the Russias by the Jewish laws from head to foot, showing that he
is the false Messiah and the false Christ, as the Sibyl prophesied about
him that a Jewish Tsar will reign. And that false Christ began to set
himself up and be called God by all, persecuting and tormenting all
Orthodox Christians, destroying their memory from the face of the
earth, spreading his new Jewish faith throughout all Russia. In the
year 1700, to the accomplishment of his wickedness, and on the festival
of the Circumcision of Christ, he called together a heathenish court
and erected a temple to the heathen god Janus, and before all the
people practiced all sorts of magic rites and all called out "vivat!
vivat! the New Year," and he sent to all parts of the realm the command to feast for the new year, thus breaking the laws of the Fathers,
who in the first Ecumenical Council commanded the feast of the New
Year to be on September 1. In the year 1721 he took upon himself the
Patriarchal title, calling himself Father of the Country, Head of the
Russian Church, and Autocrat, having no one on an equality with
himself, taking craftily to himself not only the power of the Tsar, but
also the authority of God, and claiming to be an autocratic pastor, a
headless head over all opponents of Christ, Anti-Christ. Therefore
must we conceal ourselves in the deserts just as the Prophet Jeremiah
ordered the children of God to flee from Babylon. The years of the
Lord have passed; the years of Satan have come.

MANSTEIN: INTO THE HANDS OF FOREIGNERS [8]

*General von Manstein was one of those foreigners who re-
sponded to the Petrine need for foreign military leadership, and
he spent a lifetime in Russian service.*

[8] General von Manstein, *Memoirs of Russia, Historical, Political and Military,*
Introduction by David Hume (London, 1770), pp. 391–402.

Peter I during his reign, took all the pains imaginable to make his subjects good merchants, and to engage them not to sell any longer the merchandises produced in his dominions at second hand by foreigners, but to carry on their trade directly in goods laden on Russian bottoms to foreign countries, in the manner practised by other commercial nations.

In the beginning of this century, the Emperor made a trial of this kind. He sent a Russian merchant, called Soloview, to Amsterdam, there to establish a Russian factory, or house of trade; and that he might succeed the better, he not only gave him several commissions of the court, but there were also granted to him great advantages on the rest of his trade to Russia. As Soloview was really a man of parts, and had all the necessary capacity, he knew so well how to avail himself of all these circumstances, that he had, in a few years, gained a considerable capital, at the same time that his civil behavior had won him the friendship and confidence of all the Dutch merchants. But Peter I being in 1717 in Amsterdam, some of the great men of the court, who had taken a pique against him, because he would not satisfy the extortions of their avarice, found means to blacken him in the opinion of the Emperor, who, having caused this merchant to be carried off, had him embarked on board of a ship for Russia. This occasioned the Russian trade's falling into a great decline in Holland, the dealers of Amsterdam being thereby grown afraid of trusting any Russian merchant, so that it has not since been possible to form there any solid establishment.

Peter I would try another scheme. He resolved to procure the sale of the merchandise of his empire in those states which had no direct trade with Russia, and, for that purpose, obliged some of the most substantial merchants of his country to load considerable parcels of hemp, of flax, of cables, of wax, on vessels furnished them by the admiralty: to these he added a great quantity of iron-guns, of mortars, bomb-shells, cannon-balls, and anchors, and sent all this to Bourdeaux and Cadiz, where there had been previously placed Russian consuls. But this trade succeeded so ill, that the charges of merchandise absorbed a good part of the capital, and the adventurers never saw but very little returns.

At length, this Prince flattered himself that he should inspire his subjects with a taste for trade to foreign countries, and for navigation, by publishing an edict, in which it was ordained. That if any freeman of a town would trade upon his own account, on a Russian bottom, he should have a quarter of the customs abated to him, both on exports and imports. But this produced no effect, for, during his life, there was not a merchant found to risque an undertaking upon that foot.

Among the manufactures established by Peter I that of arms is one of the most worthy of remark. Formerly, this empire had none made at home, but was obliged to have from other countries all the arms it wanted. But Peter I having levied an army, and built a fleet, judged it indispensably necessary to have arms fabricated in his dominions; and as the iron in them is of an excellent kind, there is nothing wanting but good armorers and gunsmiths. He caused to be engaged the best masters that could be found in other nations; gave them great salaries, and established two manufactures, one at Toula, a small town, situated at 180 wersts on the other side of Moscow, the other at Susterbeck, a little town, or rather village, about 27 wersts from Petersburgh.

In these two places, every thing is so well ordered, that the connoisseurs, who have seen them, agree that they are masterpieces in their kind. The whole is conducted there by water-works.

At Toula they make every thing requisite for the land-armies. The cannon and small arms are excellent, but they do not as yet excel in the cock-plates. The manufacture at Susterbeck, which was particularly designed for the supply of the marine, fell into decline during the reigns of Catherine and Peter II. The best masters, whom Peter I had procured at a vast expence from foreign countries, were dead or turned off, or dispersed. . . .

I come now to speak of the changes in the military. When Peter I came to the throne, he had hardly any other troops in his empire than the Strelitzes. This militia had been formed by the patriarch Philaret, father of the Czar Michael Feodorowitz, to curb the nobility and the great of that country. There is no comparing them to any thing so fitly as to the Janizaries; they fought in the same manner, and had much the same privileges as these have. They might amount to 40,000 men, divided into different regiments; part of them served in the guards about the Czar's person, the rest were distributed in garrison on the frontiers. Their arms consisted of musquets and sabres; their pay was not above four rubles a year (sixteen shillings), but as they had great privileges in trade, they might very well subsist on it. Even several rich citizens inrolled themselves in this body, who did no duty in time of peace, and in time of war they could easily exempt themselves from marching, by giving a competent present to the commander, and by sending a man in their room.

The militia having been raised to counterbalance the nobility, care was taken, from the very first of its institution, to place none at the head of it but soldiers of fortune, or some foreigners that had distinguished themselves in the wars of Poland. This had caused, and kept up the hatred between this body and the nobility. No gentleman would ever list in it, holding it shameful to serve persons of an inferior condition.

For a long time, Russia maintained no other troops in time of peace than this infantry. However, there were always kept collaterally in reserve, a number of colonels and other officers, of whom the greatest part were foreigners, and to whom there was allotted in time of peace a slender pay. As soon as a war was coming in, each colonel had a particular district assigned him, in which to levy men; and every village was obliged to furnish him the number specified for its contingent. Easy it is to judge that these people were ill disciplined, ill clothed, and ill armed. Indeed, they took whatever weapons came next to hand, and few had any fire-arms; the most of these had a sort of battle-ax, called in the Russian language berdish; the rest had wooden clubs. Such troops, one may readily imagine, were not capable of great services; and, accordingly, they were hardly trusted with any thing but guarding the baggage. As soon as the campaign was over, every soldier returned to his village; and if the war continued, there was a necessity of entirely new-raising the regiment for the next campaign. In short, these troops could not be compared to any but to those which the Turkish Bashaws bring into the field with them, excepting that these last are better armed, and have more courage.

All that is here said concerns only the infantry.

As to the cavalry, it was composed of the lesser nobility, and was called in Russia *Dieti Boiarsky*, or Boyars Children; they were dispersed over all the provinces where they possessed hereditary fees. At the opening of the campaign, each repaired to the general rendezvous, with a certain number of servants in proportion to his estate. These gentry had no pay, and were obliged to maintain themselves and their servants at their own expence during the whole war. Their common arms consisted in bows and arrows, sabres and half-pikes: some had also firearms; that is to say, such as could pay for them.

Such a cavalry opposed to disciplined enemies, would hardly have stood a very good chance; but the Tartars and Poles, against whom they had the oftenest to combat, were not much better in that respect than themselves, so that they might serve tolerably well.

Besides this cavalry composed of the nobility, Russia maintained some thousands of Tartars, who had submitted to this empire, on the terms of preserving their liberty of conscience, after the conquest of the kingdom of Kasan.

In the case too of the Czars, their wanting a more numerous cavalry, they could take a great number of Calmucks into their pay, to whom they paid no more than a ruble (four shillings) a year, and a mantle made of a sheep's skin.

But when the Cossacks had, at length, put themselves under the protection of Russia, its troops were augmented by a hundred thousand horses.

Among the ancient Czars, there were some that had a foreign guard; as for example, Iwan Basiliwitz, to whom the historians have given, though wrongfully, the appellation of tyrant, for he was one of the greatest men that ever Russia produced.

The Czar, Michael Feodorowitz, in the last years of his reign, and his son, Alexis Michaelowitz, had already had the design of putting the army upon another foot. During the war they had with Poland, they had formed some regiments of infantry upon the foot of other European troops, and had given the command of them to foreign officers. The regiment of Boutinsky had subsisted ever since the year 1642; one Dalziel commanded it: this regiment was composed of fifty-two companies, each of a hundred men. There are also to be seen ancient lists of the regiment of the first Moskowsky, of the year 1648; a general, Drummond, was the commander.

The Czar, Alexis Michaelowitz, caused to be translated into the Russian language, a book on the military art (which had been published in German) to serve for the instruction of his officers. He also sent for from Brescia eight thousand carabines, which are actually now at Moscow.

But as there was, at that time, a necessity for keeping measures with the Strelitzes, who beheld with a jealous eye these new troops; as the Boyars also, who had great influence at court, would not consent to lose entirely the peasants belonging to their lands, and who, according to ancient custom, were not obliged to serve but only in time of war, and then, no longer than the campaign lasted; especially too, as the clergy, who had great power, were afraid that foreign heretics might gain too great an ascendant over the sovereign; this project of reformation came to little or nothing.

It was under the reign of Alexis Michaelowitz, that about three thousand Scotch arrived in Russia, who had quitted Great Britain after the defeat and imprisonment of King Charles I. These were very well received; they had a place assigned them contiguous to the town of Moscow, where they built houses, and formed that part of this great town, which is distinguished to this day by the name of Inostranaya Sloboda, or habitation of strangers.

Peter I having ascended the throne, the various troubles with which the beginning of his reign was agitated, obliged him to put himself into the hands of foreigners, and to shake off those prejudices which had hindered his father and grandfather from executing the project of alteration they had begun. After this Prince had rid himself of the Strelitzes, his first care was to root out of the higher nobility that prejudice as to their quality, from which they held it an indignity for a man of a great birth to serve under a man of an inferior one. To succeed in this design he fell upon the following expedient. He formed out of the youths, who were brought up with him, according to the custom of that time, a company of fifty, under the name of Poteschnie (or for amusement), and made them be clothed in one uniform, and exercised in the foreign manner; declaring at the same time, that he would have no prerogative over his comrades. He began with serving in the lowest degree, not even so high as a private soldier, but in quality of drummer. He renounced all his authority as to the military rank, depositing it in trust in the hands of the Prince Romandonowsky, who was to advance him according to his merit, and without any favor: and so long as Prince Romandonowsky lived, which was till 1714, it was always he that advanced Peter I to the ranks of general and admiral, when he would take them upon him.

By this means the Emperor arrived at his end, for the nobility seeing that their master did not make any distinction of quality in the service, submitted also to the like; and though they could not forget the prerogative of their birth, they were, however, ashamed of pretending upon it to a right of which the Emperor had divested himself.

Little by little the Emperor augmented this company, and at length formed two regiments of infantry, whom he declared his guards in 1706. Blomberg was colonel of the first, and the marshal Prince Gallitzin of the second: they were clothed, armed, and exercised after the manner of the other troops of Europe. Some time afterwards he established some more regiments of infantry on the same footing, and gave orders to all his ministers at the foreign courts to engage as many officers in his service as they could find. In a few years he had a considerable number of very good ones.

The Emperor wanted also to form his cavalry upon the same foot as that of the rest of Europe. For this purpose, he took some hundreds of Saxon reysters or horsemen into his service, that were to serve for a model; but having discovered that there were not to be found in all Russia horses proper for remounting the heavy cavalry, and that, if he had recourse to foreign ones, the expences would be too great; he was obliged to abandon this project, and content himself with raising regiments of dragoons.

Among the foreigners who came to Russia, the principal was the marshal Ogilvy: it is to this general that the Russians are indebted for the first establishment of order and discipline in their army, and especially in the infantry.

As to the dragoons, it was the general Ronne, a Courlander, that was in charge of them; but as almost all the officers, and particularly the generals who entered into the service of Peter I, had never served but in the infantry; the exercises and evolutions of the cavalry were much neglected, and the dragoons learn'd no other part of the exercise than what belonged to them when dismounted to act on foot: they had scarce any knowledge of evolutions on horseback.

7
The View from Europe

BURNET: SCOURGE OF HIS NATION
AND HIS NEIGHBORS [1]

Bishop Burnet had an opportunity to observe Tsar Peter during his visit to England in 1698.

I mentioned, in the relation of the former year, the czar's coming out of his own country; on which I will now enlarge: he came this winter over to England, and stayed some months among us; I waited often on him, and was ordered, both by the king and the archbishop and bishops, to attend upon him, and to offer him such informations of our religion and constitution, as he was willing to receive; I had good interpreters, so I had much free discourse with him; he is a man of a very hot temper soon inflamed, and very brutal in his passion; he raises his natural heat, by drinking much brandy, which he rectifies himself with great application: he is subject to convulsive motions all over his body.

The king made the czar a visit, in which an odd incident happened. The czar had a favourite monkey, which sat upon the back of his chair; as soon as the king was sat down, the monkey jumped upon him in some wrath, which discomposed the whole ceremonial; and most of the time was afterwards spent in apologies for the monkey's misbehaviour. He had a great dislike to being looked at, but had a mind to see the king in parliament; in order to which, he was placed in a gutter upon the house-top, to peep in at the window; where he made so ridiculous a figure, that neither king nor people could forbear laughing; which obliged him to retire sooner than he intended.

. . . He wants not capacity, and has a larger measure of knowledge, than might be expected from his education, which was very indifferent; a want of judgment, with an instability of temper, appear in him too often and too evidently; he is mechanically turned, and seems designed by nature rather to be a ship-carpenter, than a great prince.

[1] Bishop Burnet, *History of His Own Time* (Oxford: Clarendon Press, 1823), pp. 396–98.

This was his chief study and exercise, while he stayed here: he wrought
much with his own hands, and made all about him work at the models
of ships: he told me, he designed a great fleet at Azuph, and with it
to attack the Turkish empire; but he did not seem capable of con-
ducting so great a design, though his conduct in his wars since this,
has discovered a greater genius in him than appeared at that time. He
was desirous to understand our doctrine, but he did not seem disposed
to mend matters in Moscovy; he was indeed resolved to encourage
learning, and to polish his people, by sending some of them to travel
in other countries, and to draw strangers to come and live among
them. He seemed apprehensive still of his sister's intrigues. There was
a mixture both of passion and severity in his temper. He is resolute,
but understands little of war, and seemed not at all inquisitive that
way. After I had seen him often, and had conversed much with him,
I could not but adore the depth of the providence of God, that had
raised up such a furious man to so absolute an authority over so great
a part of the world.

David, considering the great things God had made for the use of
man, broke out into the meditation, What is man, that thou art so
mindful of him? But here there is an occasion for reversing these
words, since man seems a very contemptible thing in the sight of God,
while such a person as the czar has such multitudes put as it were
under his feet, exposed to his restless jealousy and savage temper. He
went from hence to the court of Vienna, where he purposed to have
stayed some time, but he was called home sooner than he had intended, upon a discovery or a suspicion of intrigues managed by his
sister: the strangers to whom he trusted most, were so true to him,
that those designs were crushed before he came back; but on this
occasion he let loose his fury on all whom he suspected; some hundreds
of them were hanged all around Moscow, and it was said that he cut
off many heads with his own hand, and so far was he from relenting,
or shewing any sort of tenderness, that he seemed delighted with it.
How long he is to be the scourge of that nation, or of his neighbours,
God only knows: so extraordinary an incident will, I hope, justify
such a digression.

SOPHIA CHARLOTTE: A VERY EXTRAORDINARY MAN [2]

*Sophia Charlotte, wife of the elector of Brandenburg, met
Peter during the "Great Embassy" to Europe in 1697. She found
him something of a "natural savage," full of innate good sense
and good humor, but rough and ill-mannered. The first excerpt
is her report, and the second that of her daughter.*

[2] Reprinted in Schuyler, *Peter the Great*, vol. 1, pp. 348-50.

The Tsar is very tall, his features are fine, and his figure very noble. He has great vivacity of mind, and a ready and just repartee. But with all the advantages with which nature has endowed him, it could be wished that his manners were a little less rustic. We immediately sat down to table. Herr Koppenstein, who did the duty of marshal, presented the napkin to his Majesty, who was greatly embarrassed, for at Brandenburg, instead of a table napkin, they had given him an ewer and basin after the meal. He was very gay, very talkative, and we established a great friendship for each other, and he exchanged snuff boxes with my daughter. We stayed, in truth, a very long time at table, but we would gladly have remained there longer still without feeling a moment of ennui, for the Tsar was in very good humor, and never ceased talking to us. My daughter had her Italians sing. Their song pleased him, though he confessed to us that he did not care much for music.

I asked him if he liked hunting. He replied that his father had been very fond of it, but that he himself, from his earliest youth, had had a real passion for the navigation of ships, showed us his hands, and made us touch the callous places that had been caused by work. He brought his musicians, and they played Russian dances, which he liked better than Polish ones.

Lefort and his nephew dressed in French style, and had much wit. We did not speak to the other ambassadors. We regretted that he could not stay longer, so that we could see him again, for his society gave us much pleasure. He is a very extraordinary man. It is impossible to describe him, or even to give an idea of him, unless you have seen him. He has a very good heart, and remarkably noble sentiments. I must tell you, also, that he did not get drunk in our presence, but we had hardly left when the people of his suite made ample amends. . . .

I could embellish the tale of the journey of the illustrious Tsar, if I should tell you that he is sensible to the charms of beauty, but, to come to the bare fact, I found in him no disposition to gallantry. If we had not taken so many steps to see him, I believe that he would never have thought of us. In his country it is the custom for all women to paint, and rouge forms an essential part of their marriage presents. That is why Countess Platen singularly pleased the Muscovites; but in dancing, they took the whalebones of our corsets for our bones, and the Tsar showed his astonishment by saying that the German ladies had devilish hard bones.

They have four dwarfs. Two of them are very well-proportioned, and perfectly well-bred; sometimes he kissed, and sometimes he pinched the ear of his favorite dwarf. He took the head of our little princess (Sophia Dorothea) and kissed her twice. The ribbons of her hair suffered in consequence. He also kissed her brother (later George II of England). He is a prince at once very good and very *méchant*. He has quite the manners of his country. If he had received a better education, he would be an accomplished man, for he has many good qualities, and an infinite amount of natural wit. . . .

My mother and I began to pay him our compliments, but he made Mr. Lefort reply for him, for he seemed shy, hid his face in his hands, and said: "Ich kann nicht sprechen." But we tamed him a little, and then he sat down at the table between my mother and myself, and each of us talked to him in turn, and it was a strife who should have it. Sometimes he replied with the same promptitude, at others he made two interpreters talk, and assuredly he said nothing that was not to the point on all subjects that were suggested, for the vivacity of my mother put to him many questions, to which he replied with the same readiness, and I was astonished that he was not tired with the conversation, for I have been told that it is not much the habit in his country. As to his grimaces, I imagined them worse than I found them, and some are not in his power to correct. One can see also that he has had no one to teach him how to eat properly, but he has a natural, unconstrained air which pleases me.

KOLLONITZ: NOTHING WOULD DECLARE HIM TO BE A PRINCE[3]

Cardinal Kollonitz, Roman Catholic primate of Hungary, met Tsar Peter in Vienna during the tsar's visit in 1699. The cardinal, raised on the excessive court formalities of the age of the "Sun King," thought that Peter had little of royalty about him.

The Tsar is a youth of from twenty-eight to thirty years of age, is tall, of an olive complexion, rather stout than thin, in aspect between proud and grave, and with a lively countenance. His left eye, as well as his left arm and leg, was injured by the poison given him during the life of his brother; but there remain now only a fixed and fascinated look in his eye and a constant movement of his arm and leg, to hide which he accompanies this forced motion with continual movements of his entire body, which, by many people, in the countries which he has visited, has been attributed to natural causes, but really it is artificial. His wit is lively and ready; his manners rather civil

[3] Reprinted in Schuyler, *Peter the Great,* vol. 1, pp. 383–84.

than barbarous, the journey he has made having improved him, and the difference from the beginning of his travels and the present time being visible, although his native roughness may still be seen in him; but it is chiefly noticeable in his followers, whom he holds in check with great severity. He has a knowledge of geography and history, and —what is most to be noticed—he desires to know these subjects better; but his strongest inclination is for maritime affairs, at which he himself works mechanically, as he did in Holland; and this work, according to many people who have to do with him, is indispensable to divert the effects of the poison, which still very much troubles him. In person and in aspect, as well as in his manners, there is nothing which would distinguish him or declare him to be a prince.

MANTEUFFEL: IMPOSSIBLE FOR THE KING
TO KEEP UP WITH HIM [4]

Baron Manteuffel, advisor to the king in Prussia, wrote the following to Count Flemming describing Peter the Great's visit to Berlin in December, 1712, while on his way to the waters at Carlsbad.

The Tsar arrived here last Tuesday at 7 P.M. We were in the tabagie when the Field-Marshal came to inform the King, who asked me how he had been received in Dresden. I said that though the King was absent, all sorts of honours had been offered to him, but he had accepted almost nothing, and had lodged in a private house. His Majesty replied that he would likewise offer him everything. "Nimmt er's nicht an," he said, "so mag er's bleiben lassen."

The Tsar lodged with Count Golofkin, and sent him to inform the King of his arrival. The King and the Queen sent to compliment him. Half an hour later the Tsar went to the palace, and going up the private staircase surprised the King in his bedroom, playing chess with the Prince Royal. The two Majesties stayed half an hour together. Then the Tsar looked at the apartments in which the King of Denmark had stayed, admired them, but refused to occupy them. A supper was given to him by the Prince Royal, there being eight at table besides the Tsar, who allowed no toasts, ate, though he had already supped, but did not drink.

Yesterday the Tsar went to the arsenal. When about to breakfast, the King came to make a visit, and invited the Tsar to dine. The Tsar accepted, but afterwards put it off for supper. He came to see the Queen, whom he found surrounded by ladies of the city. After half an hour he went to the King in the tabagie, put on a fine red coat embroidered with gold, instead of his pelisse, which he found too hot, and went to supper. He was gallant enough to give his hand to the Queen, after having put on a rather dirty glove. The King and all the Royal Family utriusque sexus supped with him, the Golofkins, Kurakin, &c.

The Tsar surpassed himself during all this time. He neither belched, nor farted, nor picked his teeth—at least, I neither saw nor heard him do so—and he conversed with the Queen and with the Princesses without showing any embarrassment. The crowd of spectators was very great. After supper the Tsar conducted the Queen to her apartment. She, at the instigation of M. Frisendorff, took occasion to speak in favour of Rehnskjold. He said plainly that nothing was to be done, and as the Queen continued to insist, he left her, embraced the King for good-bye, and, after making a general bow to all the company, went off with such long strides that it was impossible for the King to keep up with him. At seven this morning he left for Potsdam and further.

LIBOY: VERY CHANGEABLE AND IRRESOLUTE [5]

Monsieur de Liboy, Gentleman of the Household of Louis XV, was charged with waiting upon Tsar Peter during his visit to France in 1717.

This little court is very changeable and irresolute, and from the throne to the stable very subject to anger. I persist in what I have said of the character of the Tsar, in whom one does indeed find seeds of virtue, but they are all wild and very mixed. I believe that uniformity and constancy in his projects is what fails him most, and that he has not arrived at that point when one can really rely upon what would be concluded with him. I admit that Prince Kurakin is polite; he appears to be intelligent and to desire to arrange everything to our mutual satisfaction. I do not know if it is by temperament or through fear of the Tsar, who appears, as I have said, very hard to please and quick tempered, that Kurakin seems to treat the least trifles with warmth and as very important. I will not enter into details. Prince Dolgoruky appears a gentleman, and to be much esteemed by the Tsar; the only inconvenience is that he understands absolutely no

[5] Reprinted in Vicomte de Guichen, *Pierre le Grand et le premier traité Franco-Russe* (Paris, 1908), pp. 172–74; trans. L. J. Oliva.

language but Russian. In this respect, allow me to remark that the term Muscovite, or even Muscovy, is deeply offensive to all this court. The lieutenant-general Buturlin is much esteemed by the Tsar, and understands a little German. The councillor Tolstoi is in his confidence, is very polite, and speaks Italian. The adjutant and chamberlain Yaguzhinsky is the favourite. He is fond of pleasure, and never goes to bed sober. He does not appear to take any part in affairs, and, to tell the truth, it is on Prince Kurakin that everything respecting the journey depends. You know the councillor Erskine better than I do. I think that he is very desirous of meddling in everything, and that he is shut out everywhere. The secretary Makarof has a district that I do not know, as also the secretary Volkof. They neither of them appear to be personages of importance. I have not seen the councillor Osterman, and I do not know what he does. He has been invited out several times. I think he comes seldom to table, and takes part in very little. Raguzhinsky is a thoughtless young man, and nephew of Savva Raguzhinsky, whom you have seen the last ten days in Paris, who intrigues in all sorts of affairs, and whom I think a man little to be relied upon. You know him, he is distinguished in the list. The arch-priest is the boon companion of the favourite, and at least as little sober, and a great burden. I think he busies himself only with drinking. He speaks nothing but Russian. This, Monseigneur, is what I have been able to remark up till now of the principal personages of this court. The Tsar rises early, dines about ten o'clock, sups about seven, and retires before nine. He drinks liquors before meals, beer and wine in the afternoon, sups very little, and sometimes not at all. I have not been able to perceive any sort of council or conference for serious business, unless they discuss affairs while tippling. I am even astonished, and I do not know if they do not live from hand to mouth, the Tsar deciding alone and promptly whatever is presented. This Prince varies on all occasions his amusements and walks, and is extraordinarily quick, impatient, and very hard to please. He likes especially to see the water. He lives in the great apartments, and sleeps in some out-of-the-way room if there be any. . . .

The Tsar has a head cook who prepares two or three dishes for him every day, and who uses for this purpose enough wine and meat to serve a table of eight.

He is served both a meat and a lenten dinner on Fridays and Saturdays.

He likes sharp sauces, brown and hard bread, and green peas.

He eats many sweet oranges and apples and pears.

He generally drinks light beer and dark vin de Nuits, without liquor.

The morning he drinks aniseed water (Kummel), liquors before meals, beer and wine in the afternoon. All of them fairly cold.

He eats no sweetmeats and does not drink sweetened liquors at his meals.

LEIBNIZ: A PERSON WHOM GOD HAS DESTINED TO GREAT WORKS [6]

The philosopher Leibniz was one of Peter's ardent admirers and advisers, seeing in the tsar the opportunity to implement many of his own views on society. The following letter was written after the battle of Poltava in 1709.

The Tsar henceforth will attract the consideration of Europe, and will have a very great part in general affairs. People greatly praise his humanity and his goodness in giving Swedish officers leave on parole. But he is right to keep the soldiers. He can make very good colonies of them on the frontiers of his empire. You can believe how much the revolution in the north astonished many people. It is commonly said that the Tsar will be formidable for all Europe, and will be like a northern Turk. But can he be prevented from educating his subjects and rendering them civilised and warlike? Qui jure suo utitur nemini facit injuriam. As for me, who am for the good of the human race, I am very glad that so great an empire is putting itself in the ways of reason and of order, and I consider the Tsar in that respect as a person whom God has destined to great works. He has succeeded in having good troops. I do not doubt that by your means he will succeed in also having good foreign relations, and I shall be charmed if I can help him make science flourish in his country. I maintain even that he can do in that respect finer things than all other princes have done. As for me, I am persuaded that the princes of Germany, especially those who love the maintenance of justice against the violence of the most powerful, cannot take better measures than with his Tsarish Majesty, and I hope that this prince will enter as a guarantor into the general treaty of peace.

THOMSON: IMMORTAL PETER! FIRST OF MONARCHS!

James Thomson (1700–1748) was a Scots poet whose master work, The Seasons, *appeared between 1726 and 1730. His treat-*

[6] Reprinted in Schuyler, *Peter the Great*, vol. 2, pp. 160–61.

ment of Peter in that poem helped to lay the foundations for the Petrine legend in western Europe.

What cannot active government perform,
New-moulding man? Wide stretching from these shores,
A people savage from remotest time,
A huge neglected empire, one vast mind,
By heaven inspired, from Gothic darkness call'd.
Immortal Peter! first of monarchs! He
His stubborn country tamed—her rocks, her fens,
Her floods, her seas, her ill-submitting sons;
And while the fierce barbarian he subdued,
To more exalted soul he raised the man.
Ye shades of ancient heroes, ye who toil'd
Through long successive ages to build up
A laboring plan of state, behold at once
The wonder done! Behold the matchless prince,
Who left his native throne, where reign'd till then
A mighty shadow of unreal power;
Who greatly spurned the slothful pomp of courts;
And, roaming every land, in every port
His sceptre laid aside, with glorious hand
Unwearied plying the mechanic tool;
Gather'd the seeds of trade, of useful arts,
Of civil wisdom, and of martial skill!
Charged with the stores of Europe, home he goes!
Then cities rise amid th'illumined waste;
O'er joyless deserts smiles the rural reign;
Far-distant flood to flood is social join'd;
The astonished Euxine hears the Baltic roar,
Proud navies ride on seas that never foam'd
With daring keel before; and armies stretch
Each way their dazzling files, repressing here
The frantic Alexander of the North,
And awing there stern Othman's shrinking sons.
Sloth flies the land, and Ignorance, and Vice,
Of old dishonour proud; it glows around,
Taught by the royal hand that roused the whole,
One scene of arts, of arms, of rising trade:
For what his wisdom plann'd, and power enforced,
More potent still, his great example show'd.

SAINT-SIMON: A PRODIGY [7]

The duke de Saint-Simon, premier diarist of the Regency in France, was much impressed by the tsar's visit to France in 1717 and included a detailed report based on personal observations.

       Peter I Czar of Muscovy has justly acquired such a great name in his own country and in every part of Europe and Asia that I would not undertake to introduce such a renowned and illustrious prince, a prince comparable to the great men of ancient times, who has won the admiration of this century, who will win the admiration of the centuries to come, and whom all Europe yearns so strongly to know. The amazing nature of the journey into France of a prince so extraordinary seems to me to merit being told in its entirety and without interruption. It is for this reason that I insert my narration a little later than it ought to appear in the chronology of my notes; the dates provided will rectify this fault.

       We have previously mentioned several activities of this monarch, his different travels in Holland, Germany, Vienna, England and in several parts of the north of Europe, the purpose of these voyages, something of his military actions, of his politics, and of his family. We have seen also that he had wished to come into France in the last years of the late King, who discouraged him. Since this obstacle had disappeared, the Czar wished to satisfy his curiosity about France and asked the Regent through Prince Kurakin, his ambassador here, if he might come from the Low Countries, where he was visiting, in order to see the King. . . .

       The Regent, warned of the imminent arrival of the Czar on the French seacoast, sent the entourage of the King—his horses, carriages, and wagons—with Duliboy, one of the attendants of the King of whom I have formerly spoken, to await the Czar at Dunkirk and to escort him to Paris with all of his court, and to render him the same honors as to the King himself. The Czar proposed to spent 100 days on this journey. The apartments of the Queen Mother in the Louvre were furnished for him. . . . The Duke of Orleans spoke with me concerning the titled noble whom he should select to assign to the Czar during his stay. I counselled him on the Marshal de Tessé, as a man who had little to do, who was adept in social graces and the language

[7] *Mémoires de Saint-Simon* (Paris: Hachette, 1920), vol. 21, pp. 356–87; trans. L. J. Oliva.

of the world, very much accustomed to foreigners by his war experiences and his diplomatic posts in Spain, at Turin, at Rome, and in other courts of Italy, who was gentle and polite, and who would surely do very well in the post. The Duke of Orleans thought that I was right, and the next day sent for de Tessé and gave him his orders. . . .

The Marshal de Tessé awaited the Czar for a day at Beaumont in order not to miss him. The Czar arrived there on Wednesday, May 7th at noon. Tessé paid his homage as the Czar descended from his carriage, had the honor of dining with him, and escorted him the same day to Paris. The Czar wished to enter Paris in the Marshal's carriage, and with 300 of his court, but without the Marshal in attendance. The Marshal followed him in another carriage. He arrived at the Louvre at nine o'clock in the evening and took possession of the apartments of the Queen Mother. He found the apartments too magnificent and splendid, returned to his carriage, and went to the Hotel de Lesdiguieres, where he wished to stay. There he also found the apartments which were prepared for him much too ornate and had his camp-cot put up in a dressing room. The Marshal de Tessé, who had to look after his house and his table, accompanied him everywhere and never left his side. The Marshal lived in an apartment at the Hotel de Lesdiguieres, but he had a great deal of difficulty keeping abreast of the Czar and often had to run after him. Verton, one of the servants of the King, was charged to serve the Czar and to keep table for the Czar and all of his court. About forty persons of all kinds, of whom twelve or fifteen were men of considerable rank, dined with him. Verton was a man of spirit, good cheer and great good humor, who served the Czar with so much efficiency and knew his role so well that the Czar developed a particular friendship for him as well as did most of the court.

This monarch was much admired for his curiosity; he was continually interested in matters of government, commerce, education, police, and his curiosity reached into everything and disdained nothing. The smallest display of his curiosity was marked by wisdom and good sense, for he esteemed only those things which merited to be esteemed. . . . Everything about him testified to his extraordinary intelligence. He bore himself always with the greatest majesty, with the most delicate and the most sustained pride. He maintained his majesty with complete assurance, and with an easy courtesy toward everyone. . . . He had a sort of familiarity which came from freedom, but he could not escape the strong imprint of the ancient barbarism of his country, which made all his actions quick, even precipitous, his desires uncertain; he never wished to be constrained or contradicted by anyone even though his opinions often changed.

The manners at his table were often crude and grew worse after the meal had finished, for the Czar was a bold ruler who felt himself at home everywhere. Everything that he desired to see or to do he did in his own independent manner, and it was always necessary to bow to his will. He always decided to see things at his own leisure, and hated to be made a spectacle of. His taste for freedom often led him to take rented carriages, even hackney coaches, or even a carriage belonging to those who had come to visit him and whom he did not know at all. He would leap into a carriage and have himself driven through the city or even outside it. Such an adventure happened to Madame de Maintenon, who had come to stare at him; he took her carriage to Boulogne and other places in the country and she found herself, astonished, on foot. Whenever the Czar escaped in this manner, it was the duty of the Marshal de Tessé and his assistants to pursue him, although sometimes they could not find him.

The Czar was a very large man, very well built, on the thin side, with a rounded face, a high forehead, and beautiful eyebrows; his nose was relatively short and wide at the tip, his lips rather thick and his complexion reddish and brown. He had beautiful black eyes, very large, lively, piercing and deep. When he put his mind to it he had a majestic and gracious air, but usually he was severe and rather fierce, with a tic which did not come often but which distorted his eyes and his whole face and gave him a frightening air. This frightening and terrible look would last a moment and then return to normal. Everything about him reflected his intelligence, his intellect and his grandeur and showed a certain grace. He wore only a cloth collar, a round brown wig without powder, which did not reach to his shoulders, a brown jacket with gold buttons, a vest, stockings, but never gloves or cuffs; he wore the star of his order on his coat and a cordon beneath it. His coat was often unbuttoned completely, his hat was always on the table and never on his head, even when he was outdoors. In all this simplicity, despite the common carriage he might be riding in and unaccompanied as he might be, he could not disguise the air of grandeur which was natural to him. The amount that he could eat and drink in two meals was inconceivable, and that does not count the beer, lemonade and other drinks which he and all his court drank between meals. He would average one or two bottles of beer, as much and sometimes more of wine, wines and liquors afterwards, and at the end of dinner some prepared eaux-de-vie.

His court ate and drank even more at meals which began at eleven in the morning and at eight in the evening. No matter how much food or drink was brought, it always disappeared. There was a chaplain who ate at the table of the Czar who had an appetite double anyone else's, and the Czar enjoyed him very much. Prince Kurakin went every day to the Hotel des Lesdiguieres, but he stayed at his own lodgings at night. The Czar understood French very well and, I think, would have spoken it if he had wished. But by ceremonial he always had an interpreter. He also spoke Latin and even other languages very well. At his hotel he was provided with a group of the King's guards, but he never wished to be escorted outside by them. He did not wish to leave the Hotel des Lesdiguieres despite his great curiosity, nor give any other sign of activity, until he had received the King's visit.

Saturday morning, the day after his arrival, the Regent went to see the Czar. The monarch came out of his room, took some steps toward him, embraced him with a great air of superiority, showed him to the door of his room, and turned and entered without further ceremony. The Regent followed him, and Prince Kurakin went after him to serve as interpreter. They sat in two arm chairs facing each other; the Czar seated himself in the higher one, and the Regent in the other. Their conversation lasted nearly an hour, with no business spoken of, after which the Czar left the room with the Regent behind him. The Regent made a deep bow which was indifferently returned and left by the same door by which he had entered.

The Monday following, the 10th of May, the King went to see the Czar who received him at his gate, saw him descend from his carriage, and walked next to the King into his room where they used the same two arm chairs. The King seated himself on the right, and the Czar in the one on the left; once again Prince Kurakin served as interpreter. Everyone was astonished to see the Czar take the King in his arms, lift him up in the air and embrace him. The King, despite his youth and the shock of this event, did not seem afraid. Everyone was struck by the kindliness which the Czar showed to the King, by the air of tenderness which he displayed for him, by the politeness which attested to his majesty, by the care with which he handled the differences in age. All of these things made themselves very distinctly felt. He strongly praised the King; he seemed to be charmed by him, and he persuaded everyone of it. He embraced him several times. The King gave his short speech very prettily, and Monsieur du Maine, the Marshal Villeroy, and other distinguished men who were present, provided the conversation. The meeting lasted a short quarter of an hour. The Czar accompanied the King as he had received him and watched him mount his carriage.

On Tuesday, May 11th, the Czar went to see the King between four and five o'clock. He was received by the King at the door of his carriage and escorted by him. The Czar demonstrated the same grace and the same affection for the King, and his visit was no longer than the one at which he had been received. But the crowd very much surprised him. He had been out since eight o'clock in the morning to see the Place Royale, the Place des Victoires, and the Place de Vendome, and the next day he was to see the observatory, the Gobelins factory, and the Jardin du Roi. Everywhere he enjoyed himself a great deal in examining things and asking a great number of questions. . . .

In the afternoon the Czar went to see Madame at the Palais-Royal, since she had already sent her compliments to him by means of one of her servants. With the exception of the arm chair, she received him as she would have received the King. The Duke of Orleans arrived to escort the Czar to the opera and the two of them sat alone in the Duke's box decorated with a tapestry. Some time later, the Czar asked if there was any beer. Quickly a large goblet was brought to him on a tray. The Regent took it, raised it up, and presented it to the Czar, who, with a smile and a polite bow of his head, took the goblet, drank it down and returned it to the tray which the Regent was still holding. The Regent then offered him a napkin which he used as he had used the beer, without rising, the spectacle of which astonished everyone. During the fourth act he went out to have dinner, but would not permit the Regent to leave the opera. On the day following, Saturday, he jumped into a carriage and went to see a number of interesting things at the home of some workmen.

On May 16th, the feast of Pentecost, he went to the Invalides, which he wished to see and to examine carefully. In the dining hall he ate soup with the old soldiers and shared their wine, drank to their health, slapping them on the back and calling them comrades. He admired the church, the infirmary, and the pharmacy very much. . . .

On Monday, May 17th, he dined early with the Prince Ragotzi, who had invited him, and afterward went to see Meudon, where he borrowed the King's horses in order to survey the gardens and the parks leisurely. The Prince Ragotzi accompanied him.

On Tuesday, May 18th, the Marshal d'Estrées came to see him at eight o'clock in the morning and escorted him in his carriage to his house at Issy where he entertained him at dinner and amused the Czar very much for the rest of the day with many of the things that he was doing relative to the French navy.

On Wednesday, May 19th, he visited several factories and workers. . . . On Monday, May 24th, the Czar went to the Tuileries very early, before the King had arisen. He went to the apartments of the Marshal de Villeroy, who showed him the Crown Jewels. The Czar found them more beautiful and more numerous than he had imagined. . . . From there he wished to go to see the King, who was already on his way to see him at the apartments of Villeroy. This was arranged so that the visit would not seem an official one, but merely one happening by chance. They met each other in a salon where they sat down. The King, who was holding a roll of paper in his hand, gave it to the Czar and told him that it was a map of his states. This gallantry very much pleased the Czar, whose air of politeness, friendship and affection was displayed with a majestic and elegant grace. . . .

Wednesday, the 16th of June, the Czar went on horseback to review two regiments of the guards, gendarmes, the Light Horse and the Musketeers. Only the Duke of Orleans accompanied him. On Friday, June 11th, he went from Versailles to Saint-Cyr, where he visited the household and the ladies in their classes. He was received as the King would have been received. He wished also to see Madame de Maintenon [mistress of the previous King, Louis XIV], who, to escape his curiosity, was in her bed with the curtains closed except for one which was only partly opened. The Czar entered her room and immediately opened the curtains by the windows; then suddenly turned and he opened the curtains by the bed and looked upon Madame de Maintenon as long as he pleased, saying not a word to her nor she to him, and, without making any sort of comment or courtesy, went away. She was very much astonished at this and very much embarrassed, but the late King was present no longer to protect her. The Czar returned to Paris on Saturday, June 12th. . . .

On Tuesday, June 15th, the Czar went early in the morning to the home of d'Antin at Paris. I was working that day with the Duke of Orleans, and I finished my work in a half-hour. The Duke was surprised at this and wished me to stay. I told him that it was my pleasure to see him often but not the Czar who would soon be leaving, and that I had never seen the Czar, and that I was going to the home of d'Antin in order to observe him at my ease. There would be no one there except the close friends and attendants of the Duchess, and the princesses, her daughters, who wished to observe the Czar also.

I entered the garden where the Czar was walking. Marshal de Tessé, who saw me from some distance, came up to me and wanted to present me to the Czar. I asked him not to do so and not to draw the Czar's attention to my presence, because I wished to watch him informally, to precede him or to follow him as I wished in order to observe him better, which I could not do if I were presented to him. I asked him to warn d'Antin, and with this precaution I was able to satisfy my curiosity leisurely. I discovered that he chatted easily enough, but always as if he were the master. He went into a salon where d'Antin showed him different plans and some curiosities, about which he asked several questions. It was here that I noticed the tic of which I have spoken. I asked Tessé if the tic struck him often. He

told me that it occurred several times a day, above all when he was
not being very careful to control it. Returning into the garden,
d'Antin drew his attention to the apartment and told him that the
Duchess was there with her ladies who were very anxious to meet him.
The Czar did not answer and allowed himself to be led. He walked
very casually, turning his head toward the apartment where all were
standing like sentries observing him. He looked them all over and
made only a very light inclination of his head to the crowd without
turning to all of them and walked proudly on. I think, taking into
account the manner in which he had received other women, that he
would have shown more courtesy to the women if the Duchess had not
made such a show of staring at him. He did not even bother to discover which one was the Duchess, nor the name of any of the others.
I was in the house nearly an hour and never stopped watching him.
Toward the end I saw that he noticed me; this caused me to be more
careful, in the fear that he would ask who I was. As he was about to
turn around, I went into the room where the luncheon was being laid.
D'Antin . . . had uncovered a portrait of the Czarina, which he had
placed on the fireplace of the room with some verses in her praise;
this pleased and surprised the Czar very much. He and his court
thought the portrait bore a strong resemblance to the Czarina.

The King gave the Czar two magnificent Gobelins tapestries. He
wished also to give him a beautiful sword studded with diamonds,
which he refused to accept. He, for his part, distributed about 60,000
livres to the servants of the King who had assisted him, gave d'Antin
and the Marshals d'Estrées and de Tessé his portrait studded with
diamonds, five medals of gold and eleven of silver which documented
the principal achievements of his reign. He gave a present of friendship to Verton, and asked the Regent to send a *Chargé-des-Affaires* to
his court, which the Regent promised to do.

On Sunday, the 20th of June, the Czar left and spent the night at
Livry. He was going directly to Spa where he was awaited by the
Czarina, and he did not wish to be accompanied by anyone, not even
during his departure from Paris. The luxury which he had observed
impressed him very much, but in leaving he voiced pity for the King
and for France saying that he saw with sadness that this luxury would
ultimately doom France. He was charmed by the manner in which
he had been received, by all that he had seen, by the freedom which
had been permitted to him, and expressed a great desire to closely
ally with the King of France, to which interest the Abbé Dubois and
England presented a sad obstacle which we have still great reason to
repent.

One could comment forever on this Czar so thoroughly and so
truly great, whose individuality and rare variety of so many great

talents will always make him a monarch worthy of the greatest admiration in ages to come, despite the great faults of the barbarism of his origins, of his country, and of his education. This is the reputation which he left unanimously established in France, where he is regarded as a prodigy of immense charm.

PART THREE

PETER THE GREAT IN HISTORY

The eminent historian Vasili Klyuchevsky summarized the situation well when he said that the Petrine reforms were a rock on which Russian historical opinions have divided ever since. The era of Peter the Great has served as a touchstone against which to measure succeeding eras; each generation of Russian history can be approached by analyzing its reaction to and its evaluation of the reforming tsar.

For Voltaire and his contemporaries of the eighteenth century, Peter was the first great "enlightened despot," who proved that progress could be legislated for reluctant peoples and that the forces of religion and tradition could be confronted and defeated. For Karamzin, at the beginning of the nineteenth century, Peter's work was a proof of the unconscious evils wrought by revolutionaries. During the first half of the nineteenth century, the intellectual battle of "westerner" and "slavophile" over Russia's direction and proper relationship to western Europe (represented here by Chaadayev, Belinsky, and Aksakov) was waged precisely over the salutary or destructive effects of Peter's reign. At the other end of the century, Vasili Klyuchevsky reflected the continuing ambivalence of Russian intellectuals toward Europe. At the beginning of the twentieth century, Paul Miliukov, historian and leader of Russia's parliamentary forces, found the reign of Peter central to the problems of his own times. And, naturally enough, Soviet Marxists from the individualistic Pokrovsky to the scholars of the Soviet Academy have been forced to explain Peter's astonishing reign in the light of the unfolding dialectic.

The reader, then, will find that an examination of Peter the Great's place in history is doubly rewarding; such examination tells us much about Peter and immensely more about Russian development since his time. Each generation of Russians has developed its own view of the "artisan-tsar," and in the process has revealed as much about itself as it has about Peter the Great.

8

Voltaire: Founder and Father of His Empire

Voltaire, the premier philosophe of the eighteenth-century Enlightenment, wrote a history of Peter's reign at the request of Peter's daughter, Empress Elizabeth (1741–62). Eighteenth-century historians sought moral lessons in history to guide their own times, and Voltaire found in Tsar Peter a model of his own ideal of the "enlightened despot," the ruler who seeks the natural laws of society and forcefully brings his people into conformity with them. Thus, the Petrine myth of the individual ruler of genius overturning the dark superstition and backwardness of his people was introduced into the European intellectual tradition under very distinguished auspices.[1]

Peter the Great was very tall, well built, with a noble face, lively eyes, and a hearty temperament accustomed to all kinds of exercise and every form of labor; he had a keen intelligence, which is at the center of all great talents, and this intelligence was tied to a restlessness which drove him to try everything and to do everything. He deserved an education worthy of his genius, but it was in the interest of the Princess Sophia to leave him in ignorance and to abandon him to the excesses that youth, pleasure, tradition, and his rank made all too easy. However, he had been recently married (June 1689), as had all other czars before him, to one of his subjects, the daughter of a Colonel Lopukhin. But being young and having for some time derived no other benefit from the throne than that of freeing himself to his own pleasures, the bonds of marriage did not bind him very strongly. The drinking pleasures which he enjoyed with some foreigners attracted to Moscow by Minister Golitsin did not seem to forecast that he would be a reformer. However, despite bad examples and despite his pleasures, he applied himself to the study of military art and government. The germ of a great man was already recognizable in him.

[1] Voltaire, "Histoire de l'Empire de Russie sous Pierre le Grand," *Oeuvres complètes de Voltaire* (Paris, 1878), vol. 16, pp. 442–47, 621–26; trans. L. J. Oliva.

One would hardly believe that a prince who would be seized with a frightful tremor and break out in a cold sweat and convulsions when he passed over a stream, would one day become the North's most well-known sailor. He confronted his fears by throwing himself into the sea despite his horror of the water; aversion changed to great love.

The ignorance in which he had been raised embarrassed him. By himself and nearly without teachers he learned enough German and Dutch to express himself and to write intelligibly in these two languages. The Germans and the Dutch were for him the most polished people, since they were the ones who had already formed an artistic party in Moscow which wished to sponsor the establishment of the arts in his empire and were excellent sailors which he regarded as a most necessary gift.

Such were his dispositions despite the distractions of his youth. However, he was always in fear of factions, he was always struggling to repress the turbulent spirit of the *streltsy,* he had to fight a nearly continual war against the *Crim Tatars* which was interrupted in 1689 by a truce which lasted only a short time.

In this interval Peter strengthened himself in the plan to call the arts into his country.

His father Alexei had already formed the same views, but neither good fortune nor the times assisted him; he transmitted his genius to his son, but a genius more developed, more vigorous and more confirmed against all difficulties.

Alexei had hired from Holland at great cost the ship's architect Bothler with carpenters and sailors to build a great frigate and a yacht on the Volga. They sailed down the river as far as Astrakhan, where it was planned to employ them in the construction of ships to carry on an advantageous commerce with Persia by way of the Caspian Sea. It was in this period that the revolt of Stenka Razin broke out; this rebel destroyed the two ships that he should have turned to his own uses. Razin massacred the captain, and the rest of the crews saved themselves by fleeing to Persia and escaping by way of the Dutch East India Company. One master carpenter, an excellent builder, remained in Russia but he was ignored for a long time.

Peter was walking one day in Ismailov, one of the palaces of his grandfather, and saw among some antiques a little English sloop that had been completely abandoned. He asked the German Timmerman, his teacher in mathematics, why this little boat was constructed in a different manner than those which he had seen on the River Moscow. Timmerman answered that the boat had been built to tack against the wind. The young prince wished to try it immediately but it was necessary to restore the boat first. They sought out the former builder, Brant, who was living in retirement in Moscow, and he put the little boat in good condition and set it on the River Yauza which flowed through the suburbs of the city.

Peter had his boat transported to a large lake in the neighborhood of the Trinity Monastery; here also he had Brant build two frigates and three yachts and even made him the pilot of these vessels. Finally, some time after, in 1694, he went to Archangel. Having had Brant construct a little ship in this port, he sailed on the Northern Sea which no Russian sovereign before him had ever seen. He was escorted by a Dutch vessel of war commanded by Captain Jolsen, and followed by all the merchant ships then docked in Archangel. Already he was learning to maneuver, and, despite the pressure on members of the court to imitate their master, he was the only one who ever learned it.

It was no less difficult to form an army which was well regulated and disciplined than it was to form a navy. His first attempts at a navy on the lake, before his journey to Archangel, seemed only the amusements of the childhood of a man of genius; and his first attempts to form an army also seemed mere amusement. This was during the regency of Sophia, and if one had suspected his games to be serious it would have been very sad for him.

He placed his confidence in a foreigner, the celebrated Lefort. Lefort was from an ancient and noble family of Piedmont who had lived for nearly two centuries in Geneva where they had become a family of the first rank. His family wished to raise him as a merchant, the normal trade of this city which was previously known for its controversies. His genius, which destined him to greater things, forced him to leave his father's house at the age of fourteen. He served four months as a cadet in the citadel of Marseilles, and from there went into Holland and spent some time as a soldier and was wounded in the siege of Grave on the Meuse, a very strong city which the Prince of Orange, later King of England, retook from Louis XIV in 1674. Seeking his advancement anywhere that his hopes would lead him, he left for Russia in 1675 with a German colonel named Verstin, who was commissioned by the Czar Alexei, father of Peter, to raise some soldiers in the Low Countries and to bring them to the port of Archangel. But when they arrived, after enduring all kinds of sea perils, Czar Alexei was dead and the government had changed. Russia was troubled. The governor of Archangel left Verstin and Lefort for a long time in great misery and threatened to send them into the depths of Siberia. Each one saved himself as well as he could. Lefort, lacking everything, went to Moscow and presented himself to the Danish resident Horn who made him his secretary. Lefort learned the Russian language, and some time after he found a way to be presented to Czar Peter. The older Ivan did not attract him, but Peter seemed more to his taste and gave him an infantry company to command.

Lefort had hardly any military experience, he was no intellectual, he had studied no particular art in any depth, but he was extremely clear sighted. The similarities between his mind and the mind of the Czar was the key to his success. He knew Dutch and German, which Peter learned as the languages of the two nations which could be most useful to his plans. Everything tended to make Lefort agreeable to Peter. The Czar attached himself to him; attraction began the favor which Lefort enjoyed and talents confirmed it.

Lefort was confidently dedicated to the most dangerous plan which a Czar could form, that of one day breaking the power of the *streltsy*. Such an attempt had cost the life of the Grand Sultan Osman, who attempted to reform the Janissaries. Peter, young as he was, threw himself into this task with more skill than Osman. At first he formed a company of fifty of his youngest servants at his country palace in Preobrazhensky. Some children of Boyars were chosen to be officers, but in order to teach these Boyars a discipline that they did not yet understand, he made them pass through all the ranks and himself gave the example by serving first as drummer-boy, then as soldier, sergeant, and lieutenant in the company. Nothing was more extraordinary nor more useful. The Russians had always made war as we used to in the times of feudal government when lords without experience led badly armed vassals without discipline into combat. This crude method, useful against armies built in a similar way, was completely powerless against regular troops.

This company formed by Peter was soon very numerous and became the Preobrazhensky Regiment of the Guards. Another company formed on this model came to be the Semenovsky Regiment of the Guards.

Peter had created, therefore, a regiment of five thousand men on whom he could count. The regiment was led by General Gordon, a Scot, and officered almost completely by foreigners. Lefort, who had borne arms for such a short time but who was capable of learning everything, undertook the task of raising a regiment of twelve thousand more men and did so. Five colonels were established under him; he found himself suddenly a general of this little army which was effectively raised against the *streltsy* as much as against the foreign enemies of the state. It should be noted, and this should confound immediately the fearful error of those who pretend that the revocation of the Edict of Nantes and its consequences had cost little in terms of manpower in France, that one third of this army, called a regiment, was composed of French refugees. Lefort exercised his new troops as if he had never had any other profession.

Peter wished to see one of these new military fortifications which were introduced for practice in time of peace. He had a fort constructed, which a part of his new troops was obliged to defend and which the other part was obliged to attack. The difference between these maneuvers and others was that in place of the pretense of combat here there was real combat in which soldiers were killed and very many were wounded. Lefort, who commanded the attack, received a serious wound. These bloody games began to worry the troops. The Czar mixed these military games with his work on the navy, and just as he had made Lefort a land general before he had even learned to command, so also he made him an admiral before he had ever sailed a vessel. But the Czar considered Lefort worthy of both honors. But it was true that the admiral was without a fleet and the general had no army except his own regiment.

Little by little the primary abuses of the military were reformed— this system of independent Boyars who led an army of militia composed of their own peasants. Such had been the former system of the Franks, the Huns, the Goths, and the Vandals, conquering peoples of the Roman Empire in its decay, and a system which would have been exterminated if it had been pitted against the ancient disciplined legions of Rome or armies such as those which exist in our own day. . . .

Peter, on return from his expedition into Persia (1722), saw himself more than ever the arbiter of the North. He declared himself protector of the family of King Charles XII who had been his enemy for eighteen years. He brought to his court the Duke of Holstein, nephew of Charles XII of Sweden, and announced his engagement to Peter's eldest daughter and was prepared from that time on to maintain his rights over the duchy of Holstein. He even concluded a treaty of alliance with Sweden.

He pursued the works which he had begun across the full extent of his states, even to the farthest point of Kamchatka. And in order to perfect his reforms he established his Academy of Sciences at Petersburg. The arts flourished on every side; manufacturers were encouraged, the navy was increased, the armies were well trained, the laws were obeyed. And Peter enjoyed his glory in peace. He wished to share his glory in a special way with the one who had shared the unhappiness of the campaign of the Pruth and whom he said had contributed substantially to the achievements of his reign.

He ordered the coronation and the anointing of his wife Catherine at Moscow in the presence of the Duchess of Courland, daughter of his eldest brother, and of the Duke of Holstein whom he was going to make his son-in-law. The published declaration merits our attention: it recalled the usage of several Christian kings in the coronation of their wives and the examples of the Emperors Basilides, Justinian, Heraclius, and Leo the Philosopher. The Emperor Peter then specified the services rendered to the state by Catherine, above all in the war against the

Turks when his outnumbered army, reduced to 22,000 men, had to fight more than 200,000. He never said in this document that the Empress ought to reign after him, but by this ceremony he prepared minds unused to this idea.

The evidence that perhaps Catherine should have been regarded as destined to mount the throne after her husband is that he himself marched before her on foot on the day of coronation, acting as a captain of the new company that he had created under the name of the Knights of the Empress. When they arrived at the church Peter himself placed the crown on her head. She wished to embrace his knees but he prevented her, and on leaving the cathedral he carried the sceptre and the globe before her. The ceremony was completely worthy of an Emperor. Peter insisted upon as much magnificence in public occasions as he insisted on simplicity in his own private life.

Having crowned his wife he was resolved to give his eldest daughter, Anna Petrovna, in marriage to the Duke of Holstein. This princess has many of the traits of her father: she was majestically tall and a great beauty. She had been engaged to the Duke of Holstein but without great ceremony. Peter already felt his health greatly altered, and a domestic sadness, which perhaps aggravated still more the malady from which he died, made these last days of his life inconvenient for pomp and ceremonials.

Catherine had a young chamberlain, named Mons de la Croix, born in Russia of a Flemish family. He was a very distinguished figure; his sister Madame Debalc, was a lady-in-waiting of the Empress and both had a prominent place in her house. Both were accused and put in prison on the accusation of having received bribes [Voltaire omits the crime of adultery and accepts the accusation that was invented in order to save the czar]. It had been forbidden since 1714 for any man of position to receive gifts under pain of punishment and death, and this instruction had been renewed several times. The brother and sister were convicted. All those who had bought or rewarded their services were named in the condemnation except the Duke of Holstein and his minister the Count of Bassevitz. It is true that some of the presents made by this Prince to those who had helped arrange his marriage were not regarded as a criminal offense.

Mons was condemned to be beheaded, and his sister, a favorite of the Empress, to receive eleven strokes of the knout. The two sons of this woman, one a chamberlain and the other a page, were degraded and sent into the army in Persia as simple soldiers.

These severe punishments, which revolt our own attitudes, were perhaps necessary in a country where the maintenance of law seemed to demand a frightful rigor. The Empress asked pardon for her lady-in-waiting but her husband angrily refused. He broke a piece of Venetian glass in his anger and said to his wife: "You see that all it requires is a blow of my hand in order to return this glass into the dust from which it was made." Catherine, looking upon it with a tender sadness, said to him: "Ah well, you have broken that which was an ornament of your palace. Do you now believe that it will become more beautiful?" These words appeased the Emperor, but all the relief which his wife could obtain was that her lady-in-waiting would receive only five blows of the knout in place of eleven.

I would not report this incident if it was not attested to by a minister who was an eyewitness and who himself had made presents to the brother and sister and was perhaps one of the principal causes of their unhappiness. This was an adventure which encouraged those who wished to believe, in their own malignity, that Catherine hated every day with the husband whose anger inspired nothing but fear in her.

These suspicions seemed confirmed by the haste with which Catherine recalled her lady-in-waiting immediately after the death of her husband and the favor which she extended to her. The duty of a historian is to report these public rumors which have been spread in our own time and in all the states of Europe at the death of this Princess struck down by a premature death, as if nature would not ultimately destroy us all. But a duty exists for the historian also to show that these rumors were deceptive and unjust.

There is an immense distance between the trifling discontent which a severe husband can produce and the desperate resolution to poison a husband and master to whom one owes everything. The danger of such an enterprise would be as great as the crime itself. There was a very large party which opposed Catherine and preferred the son of the unfortunate Tsarevich. However, neither this faction nor any man at the court suspected Catherine, and the vague rumors which ran through the court were only the opinions of some foreigners who were badly informed and who enjoyed with no reason the unhappy pleasure of ascribing great crimes to those whom they thought interested in committing them. Even this interest was very doubtful in Catherine, for it was by no means sure that she would succeed to the throne; she had been crowned, but only in the quality of wife of the sovereign and not as sovereign after him.

The declaration of Peter ordered this ceremony as a ceremony only and not as a guarantee of the right to rule. It recalled the example of Roman Emperors who had crowned their wives, and none of them had become mistress of the empire. Finally, in the time of Peter's final sickness, several people thought that the Princess Anna Petrovna would succeed him jointly with the Duke of Holstein, her husband, or that the

Emperor would name his grandson as his successor. Thus, far from Catherine having an interest in the death of the Emperor, she had every reason to wish to see him live.

Peter constantly and over a long period suffered attacks of an abscess and of a retention of urine which caused him great pain. The mineral waters of Olonitz and others that he favored could provide him no relief. He grew obviously weaker from the beginning of the year 1724. His labors, from which he never relaxed, simply accelerated his illness and hastened his end. Soon his condition seemed fatal. He resisted the treatments of hot waters which continually threw him into a nearly delirious state. He wished to write in the few moments which were left him between his pains, but his hand formed only unreadable characters in which one could only decipher the words in Russian: "Leave all to. . . ."

He cried out that the Princess Anna Petrovna should come to his bedside, for he wished to dictate to her. But when she appeared by his bed, he had already lost the ability to speak and fell into his death agony which lasted sixteen hours. The Empress Catherine had not left his side for three nights. He finally died in her arms on the 28th of January at about four o'clock in the morning.

They carried his body into the great hall of the palace followed by all the members of the Imperial family, the Senate, all the persons of the first rank, and a great crowd of people. He was exposed on a parade mount and everyone was free to approach and to kiss the hand up to the day of his burial which was accomplished on March 10/21, 1725.

It has been believed, indeed it has been printed, that he named his wife Catherine as heir to the empire in his will, but the truth is that he never made a will or at least that none has been discovered. Such astonishing negligence in a legislator only proves that he did not believe his malady to be fatal.

No one knew at the hour of his death who would take his place. He left Peter, his grandson, born of the unfortunate Alexei; he left his oldest daughter, the Duchess of Holstein. There was a considerable faction in favor of the young Peter. Prince Menshikov, bound closely to the Empress Catherine over a very long time diverted all these parties and frustrated all their plans. Peter was dying when Menshikov brought the Empress into a room where their friends were already assembled. They brought the court treasure to the fortress and bribed the guards regiments. Prince Menshikov then won over the Archbishop of Novgorod. Catherine held a secret meeting with them, with a secretary in their confidence named Macarov, and with the Minister of the Duke of Holstein.

The Empress, emerging from this council, returned to her dying husband who then took his last breaths in her arms. As soon as the senators and the general officers had gathered in the palace, the Empress addressed them. Menshikov responded in their name. For the sake of form, they then deliberated outside the presence of the Empress. The Archbishop of Plescov, Theofan, declared that the Emperor had said, on the eve of the coronation of Catherine, that she was being crowned in order that she might reign after him. All the assembly signed the proclamation and Catherine succeeded to her husband in the very hour of his death.

The death of Peter the Great was regretted in Russia by all those whom he had created, and the generation which followed that of the partisans of the ancient ways regarded him as its father. When the foreigners around him had seen that all his creations were durable, they developed a persistent admiration for him and swore that they had been inspired by his extraordinary wisdom as well as by his attempt to do astonishing things. Europe has recognized that he loved glory but that he struggled to do good, that his faults never overcame his great qualities, that although his faults were many he was always a great monarch. He fought against the nature of things everywhere, in his subjects, in himself, and on land and sea; but he fought against nature in order to recreate it. The arts, which he had transplanted by his own hand into lands which had been savage, have by their development given witness to his genius and made his memory eternal. They appear today to be native in areas where he had transported them. Laws, tradition, politics, military discipline, the navy, commerce, manufactures, the sciences, the fine arts, all were protected and nurtured according to his plans. And, with a steadfastness of which there is no parallel in history, four women have since mounted the Russian throne after him and have maintained all that he achieved and have perfected all that he undertook.

The palace witnessed revolutions after his death, but the state has suffered none. The splendor of this empire has grown under Catherine I; it has triumphed over the Turks and the Swedes under Anna Petrovna; it has conquered Prussia and part of Pomerania under Elizabeth; it has enjoyed peace and has seen the arts flourish under Catherine II. It is for national historians to provide all the details of the foundations, the laws, the wars, and the enterprises of Peter the Great. They will encourage their compatriots by praising all those who assisted this monarch in his military and political works. It is enough for a foreigner, and a disinterested amateur of some talent, to have tried to depict this great man who learned from Charles XII in order to conquer him, who twice left his states in order to govern them better, who worked with his hands in nearly all the necessary arts in order to give an example to his people, and who was the founder and the father of his empire.

The sovereigns of states long since organized and unified will say to themselves: "If in the glacial climates of ancient Scythia, a man, aided by his talent alone, has done such great things, what ought we to be able to do in kingdoms in which the accumulated works of several centuries have made everything easy?"

9

Karamzin: Tears and Corpses

Nicholas M. Karamzin (1766–1826), Russia's first popu-
larly read novelist and historian, was also the first major figure
to call into question the beneficial character of the Petrine era
and to undermine the solid eighteenth-century foundations of
the Petrine myth. Karamzin had been a close observer of the
revolutionary fury unleashed by France after 1789, and was
shocked by its results. He saw in the work of Peter the Great a
similar revolutionary attack on Muscovite traditional values and
evolutionary development, and began to see Peter as a subverter
of the organic nature and values of Russian society. Karamzin's
Memoir, from which the following selection is taken, was sent to
Tsar Alexander I in 1811 in order to counteract the contemplated
reforms of his own era.[1]

At this point Peter appeared. In his childhood, the license of
the lords, the impudence of the Streltsy, and the ambition of Sophia
had reminded Russia of the unhappy times of boyar troubles. But
deep inside of him the youth already had the makings of a great man,
and he seized hold of the helm of state with a mighty hand. He strove
toward his destination through storms and billows. He reached it—
and everything changed!

His goal was not only to bring new greatness to Russia, but also to
accomplish the complete assimilation of European customs. . . . Posterity has praised passionately this immortal sovereign for his personal
merits as well as for his glorious achievements. He was magnanimous
and perspicacious, he had an unshakable will, vigor, and a virtually
inexhaustible supply of energy. He reorganized and increased the
army, he achieved a brilliant victory over a skillful and courageous
enemy, he conquered Livonia, he founded the fleet, built ports, pro-
mulgated many wise laws, improved commerce and mining, established

[1] *Karamzin's Memoir on Ancient and Modern Russia,* translation and analysis
by Richard Pipes (Cambridge, Mass.: Harvard University Press, 1959), pp. 120–27.
Copyright, 1959, by the President and Fellows of Harvard College. Reprinted by
permission of the publisher.

factories, schools, the academy, and, finally, he won for Russia a position of eminence in the political system of Europe. And speaking of his magnificent gifts, shall we forget the gift which is perhaps the most important of all in an autocrat: that of knowing how to use people according to their ability? Generals, ministers, or legislators are not accidentally born into such and such a reign—they are chosen. . . . To choose good men one must have insight; only great men have insight into men. Peter's servants rendered him remarkable assistance on the field of battle, in the Senate, and in the Cabinet. But shall we Russians, keeping in mind our history, agree with ignorant foreigners who claim that Peter was the founder of our political greatness? . . . Shall we forget the princes of Moscow, Ivan I, Ivan III, who may be said to have built a powerful state out of nothing, and —what is of equal importance—to have established in it firm monarchical authority? Peter found the means to achieve greatness—the foundation for it had been laid by the Moscow princes. And, while extolling the glory of this monarch, shall we overlook the pernicious side of his brilliant reign?

Let us not go into his personal vices. But his passion for foreign customs surely exceeded the bounds of reason. Peter was unable to realize that the national spirit constitutes the moral strength of states, which is as indispensable to their stability as is physical might. This national spirit, together with the faith, had saved Russia in the days of the Pretenders. It is nothing else than respect for our national dignity. By uprooting ancient customs, by exposing them to ridicule, by causing them to appear stupid, by praising and introducing foreign elements, the sovereign of the Russians humbled Russian hearts. Does humiliation predispose a man and a citizen to great deeds? The love of the fatherland is bolstered by those national peculiarities which the cosmopolite considers harmless, and thoughtful statesmen beneficial. Enlightenment is commendable, but what does it consist of? The knowledge of things which bring prosperity; arts, crafts, and sciences have no other value. The Russian dress, food, and beards did not interfere with the founding of schools. Two states may stand on the same level of civil enlightenment although their customs differ. One state may borrow from another useful knowledge without borrowing its manners. These manners may change naturally, but to prescribe statutes for them is an act of violence, which is illegal also for an autocratic monarch. The people, in their original covenant with the king, had told them: "Guard our safety abroad and at home, punish criminals, sacrifice a part to save the whole." They had not said: "Fight the innocent inclinations and tastes of our domestic life." In this realm, the sovereign may equitably act only by example, not by decree.

Human life is short, and the rooting of new customs takes time. Peter confined his reform to the gentry. Until his reign all Russians, from the plough to the throne, had been alike insofar as they shared certain features of external appearance and of customs. After Peter, the higher classes separated themselves from the lower ones, and the Russian peasant, burgher, and merchant began to treat the Russian gentry as Germans, thus weakening the spirit of brotherly national unity binding the estates of the realm.

Over the centuries the people had become accustomed to treat the boyars with the respect due to eminent personages. They bowed with genuine humbleness when, accompanied by their noble retinues, with Asiatic splendor, to the sound of tambourines, the boyars appeared in the streets on their way to church or to the sovereign's council. Peter did away with the title of boyar. He had to have ministers, chancellors, presidents! The ancient, glorious Duma gave way to the Senate, the prikazy were replaced by colleges, the diaki by secretaries, and so it went. Reforms which made just as little sense for Russians were introduced into the military hierarchy: generals, captains, lieutenants took the place of voevody, sotniki, piatidesiatniki, and so forth. Imitation became for Russians a matter of honor and pride.

Family customs were not spared by the impact of the tsar's activity. The lords opened up their homes; their wives and daughters emerged from the impenetrable teremy; men and women began to mingle in noise-filled rooms at balls and suppers; Russian women ceased to blush at the indiscreet glances of men, and European freedom supplanted Asiatic constraint. . . . As we progressed in the acquisition of social virtues and graces, our families moved into the background; for when we have many acquaintances we feel less need of friends, and sacrifice family ties to social obligations.

I neither say nor think that the ancient Russians who had lived under the grand princes or the tsars were in all respects superior to us. We excel them not only in knowledge, but also in some ways morally; that is to say, we are sometimes overcome with shame by things which left them indifferent, and which indeed are depraved. However, it must be admitted that what we gained in social virtues we lost in civic virtues. Does the name of a Russian carry for us today the same inscrutable force which it had in the past? No wonder. In the reigns of Michael and of his son, our ancestors, while assimilating many advantages which were to be found in foreign customs, never lost the conviction that an Orthodox Russian was the most perfect citizen and Holy Rus' the foremost state in the world. Let this be called a delusion. Yet how much it did to strengthen patriotism and the moral fibre of the country! Would we have today the audacity, after having spent over a century in the school of foreigners, to boast of our civic pride? Once upon a time we used to call all other Europeans infidels; now we call them brothers. For whom was it easier to conquer Russia —for infidels or for brothers? That is, whom was she likely to resist better? Was it conceivable in the reigns of Michael and Fedor for a Russian lord, who owed everything to his fatherland, gaily to abandon his tsar forever, in order to sit in Paris, London, or Vienna, and calmly read in newspapers of the perils confronting our country? We became citizens of the world but ceased in certain respects to be the citizens of Russia. The fault is Peter's.

He was undeniably great. But he could have exalted himself still higher, had he found the means to enlighten Russians without corrupting their civic virtues. Unfortunately, Peter, who was badly brought up and surrounded by young people, met and befriended the Genevan Lefort. This man, whom poverty had driven to Moscow, quite naturally found Russian customs strange, and criticized them in Peter's presence, while lauding to high heaven everything European. The free communities of the German settlement, which delighted the untrammeled youth, completed the work of Lefort, and the ardent monarch with his inflamed imagination, having seen Europe, decided to transform Russia into Holland.

National inclinations, habits, and ideas were still sufficiently strong to compel Peter, in spite of his theoretical liking for intellectual liberty, to resort to all the horrors of tyranny in order to restrain his subjects, whose loyalty, in fact, was unquestionable. The Secret Chancery of the Preobrazhenskoe operated day and night. Tortures and executions were the means used to accomplish our country's celebrated reform. Many perished for no other crime than the defense of the honor of Russian caftans and beards, which they refused to give up, and for the sake of which they dared to reproach the monarch. These unfortunates felt that by depriving them of their ancient habits Peter was depriving them of the fatherland itself.

The extraordinary efforts of Peter reflect all the strength of his character and of autocratic authority. Nothing frightened him. The Russian church had had since time immemorial its head, first in the person of the Metropolitan, and lastly in that of the Patriarch. Peter proclaimed himself the head of the church, abolishing the Patriarchate as dangerous to unlimited autocracy. But, let us here note, our clergy had never contended against secular authority, either princely or tsarist. Its function had been to serve the latter as a useful tool in affairs of state, and as a conscience at times when it occasionally left the path of virtue. Our primate had one right: not to act, not to rebel, but to preach the truth to the sovereigns—a right which carries blessings not only for the people, but also for the monarch whose happiness consists in justice. From Peter's time on the Russian clergy had deteriorated. Our primates turned into mere sycophants of the tsars, whom they eulogized in biblical language from the pulpits. For eulogies we have poets and courtiers. The clergy's main duty is to instruct the people in virtue, and the effectiveness of this instruction depends on the respect which the clergy commands. If the sovereign presides over the assembly of the chief dignitaries of the church, if he judges them and rewards them with secular distinctions and benefits, then the church becomes subordinated to secular authority, and loses its sacred character. Its power of appeal weakens, and so does faith, and with the weakening of the faith the sovereign deprives himself of the means with which to govern the hearts of the people on extraordinary occasions, when it is necessary to forget everything, to abandon everything for the sake of the fatherland, and when the only reward which the spiritual shepherds can promise is the crown of martyrdom. Spiritual authority ought to have a separate sphere of action, apart from secular authority, but it should function in close union with it. I have in mind the realms of justice and law. Where the welfare of the state is involved, a wise monarch shall always find a way of reconciling his will with that of the metropolitan or the patriarch. But it is better for this conciliation to appear as an act of free choice and of inner persuasion than of obvious humility. An overt, complete dependence of spiritual authority on secular authority derives from the assumption that the former is useless, or, at any rate, not essential to political stability—an assumption thoroughly disproven by the experience of ancient Russia and of contemporary Spain.

Shall we close our eyes to yet another glaring mistake of Peter the Great? I mean his founding a new capital on the northern frontier of the state, amidst muddy billows, in places condemned by nature to barrenness and want. Since at that time he controlled neither Riga nor Reval, he might have founded on the shores of the Neva a commercial city for the import and export of merchandise; but the idea of establishing there the residence of our sovereigns was, is, and will remain a pernicious one. How many people perished, how much money and labor was expended to carry out this intent? Truly, Petersburg is founded on tears and corpses. A foreign traveler, upon entering a country, usually looks for its capital in localities which are most fertile and most propitious for life and health. In Russia, he sees beautiful plains, enriched with all the beauties of nature, shaded by groves of linden trees and oaks, traversed by navigable rivers whose banks please the eye and where, in a moderate climate, the salutary air favors long life. He sees all this, and regretfully turning his back on these beautiful regions, enters sands, marshes, sandy pine forests, where poverty, gloom, and disease hold sway. This is the residence of the Russian sovereigns, who must strive to the utmost to keep the courtiers and guards from starving to death, as well as to make good the annual loss of inhabitants with newcomers, future victims of premature death! Man shall not overcome nature!

But a great man demonstrates his greatness with his very errors. They are difficult if not impossible to undo, for he creates the good and the bad alike forever. Russia was launched on her new course with a mighty hand; we shall never return to bygone times! It would have taken another Peter the Great at least twenty or thirty years to establish the new order much more firmly than all the successors of Peter I up to the time of Catherine II had done. Notwithstanding his marvelous diligence, Peter left much to be finished by his successors. Menshikov, however, was concerned only with his personal ambition, and so were the Dolgorukis. Menshikov intrigued to pave the road to the throne for his son, while the Dolgorukis and Golitsyns wanted to see the pale shadow of a monarch on the throne, and to rule themselves in the name of the Supreme Council. Impudent and dastardly plots! Pygmies contending for the legacy of a giant. The aristocracy, the oligarchy was ruining the fatherland. . . . And could Russia at this time have dispensed with monarchy, after she had changed her time-sanctioned customs, and undergone internal disorders as a result of new, important reforms which, by dissociating the customs of the gentry from those of the people, had weakened spiritual authority? Autocracy became more essential than ever for the preservation of order.

10
Chaadayev: The Great Man Who Civilized Us

Peter Y. Chaadayev (1793–1856) introduced the most strenuous intellectual debate in nineteenth-century Russian thought, and in this debate the role of Peter the Great was of central importance. Russian intellectuals, faced with a rising wave of western European influences in all aspects of life, struggled to define Russian civilization and to sort out their proper relationship to "the west." Chaadayev represented the most radical "westerner" attitude in his insistence that Peter the Great had brought Russia into the stream of universal history, that only in his era did Russia begin to produce a civilization worthy of respect, and that western Europe was the proper model for Russian development. For his scorn of the Muscovite past, Chaadayev was declared insane; in 1837 he produced the "Apology of a Madman" from which the following selection is taken.[1]

For three hundred years Russia has aspired to consort with Occidental Europe; for three hundred years she has taken her most serious ideas, her most fruitful teachings, and her most vivid delights from there. For over a century Russia has done better than that. One hundred and fifty years ago the greatest of our kings—the one who supposedly began a new era, and to whom, it is said, we owe our greatness, our glory, and all the goods which we own today—disavowed the old Russia in the face of the whole world. He swept away all our institutions with his powerful breath; he dug an abyss between our past and our present, and into it he threw pell mell all our traditions. He himself went to the Occidental countries and made himself the smallest of men, and he came back to us so much the greater; he prostrated himself before the Occident, and he arose as our master and our ruler. He introduced Occidental idioms into our language; he

[1] Peter Y. Chaadayev, "Apology of a Madman," in Hans Kohn, ed., *The Mind of Modern Russia* (New York: Harper and Brothers, 1962), pp. 50–57; originally published by Rutgers University Press, 1955, and reprinted with permission of Rutgers University Press.

called his new capital by an Occidental name; he rejected his hereditary title and took an Occidental title; finally, he almost gave up his
own name, and more than once he signed his sovereign decrees with
an Occidental name.

Since that time our eyes have been constantly turned towards the
countries of the Occident; we did nothing more, so to speak, than to
breathe in the emanations which reached us from there, and to nourish
ourselves on them. We must admit that our princes almost always
took us by the hand, almost always took the country in tow, and the
country never had a hand in it; they themselves prescribed to us the
customs, the language, and the clothing of the Occident. We learned
to spell the names of the things in Occidental books. Our own history
was taught to us by one of the Occidental countries. We translated the
whole literature of the Occident, we learned it by heart, and we
adorned ourselves with its tattered garment. And finally, we were
happy to resemble the Occident, and proud when it consented to count
us as one of its own.

We have to agree, it was beautiful, this creation of Peter the Great,
this powerful thought that set us on the road we were to travel with
so much fanfare. It was a profound wisdom which told us: That civilization over there is the fruit of so much labor; the sciences and the
arts have cost so much sweat to so many generations! All that can be
yours if you cast away your superstitions, if you repudiate your prejudices, if you are not jealous of your barbaric past, if you do not
boast of your centuries of ignorance, if you direct your ambition to
appropriating the works of all the peoples and the riches acquired by
the human spirit in all latitudes of the globe. And it is not merely for
his own nation that this great man worked. These men of Providence
are always sent for the good of mankind as a whole. At first one people
claims them, and later they are absorbed by the human race, like those
great rivers which first fertilize the countryside and then pay their
tribute to the waters of the ocean. Was the spectacle which he presented to the universe upon leaving his throne and his country to go
into hiding among the last ranks of civilized society anything else but
the renewed effort of the genius of this man to free himself from the
narrow confines of his fatherland and to establish himself in the great
sphere of humanity?

That was the lesson we were supposed to learn. In effect we have
profited from it, and to this very day we have walked along the path
which the great emperor traced for us. Our immense development is
nothing more than the realization of that superb program. Never was
a people less infatuated with itself than the Russian people, such as
it has been shaped by Peter the Great, and never has a people been

more successful and more glorious in its progress. The high intelligence of this extraordinary man guessed exactly the point of our departure on the highway of civilization and the intellectual movement of the world. He saw that lacking a fundamental historical idea, we should be unable to build our future on that impotent foundation. He understood very well that all we could do was to train ourselves, like the peoples of the Occident, to cut across the chaos of national prejudices, across the narrow paths of local ideas, and out of the rusty rut of native customs; that we had to raise ourselves, by one spontaneous outburst of our internal powers, by an energetic effort of the national conscience, to the destiny which has been reserved for us. Thus he freed us from previous history which encumbers ancient societies and impedes their progress; he opened our minds to all the great and beautiful ideas which are prevalent among men; he handed us the whole Occident, such as the centuries have fashioned it, and gave us all its history for our history, and all its future for our future.

Do you not believe that if he had found in his country a rich and fertile history, living traditions, and deep-rooted institutions, he would have hesitated to pour them into a new mold? Do you not believe that faced with a strongly outlined and pronounced nationality, his founding spirit would have demanded that that nationality itself become the necessary instrument for the regeneration of his country? On the other hand, would the country have suffered being robbed of its past and a new one, a European one, being put in its place? But that was not the case. Peter the Great found only a blank page when he came to power, and with a strong hand he wrote on it the words Europe and Occident: from that time on we were part of Europe and of the Occident.

Don't be mistaken about it: no matter how enormous the genius of this man and the energy of his will, his work was possible only in the heart of a nation whose past history did not imperiously lay down the road it had to follow, whose traditions did not have the power to create its future, whose memories could be erased with impunity by an audacious legislator. We were so obedient to the voice of a prince who led us to a new life because our previous existence apparently did not give us any legitimate grounds for resistance. The most marked trait of our historical physiognomy is the absence of spontaneity in our social development. Look carefully, and you will see that each important fact in our history is a fact that was forced on us; almost every new idea is an imported idea. But there is nothing in this point of view which should give offense to the national sentiment; it is a truth and has to be accepted. Just as there are great men in history, so there are great nations which cannot be explained by the normal laws of reason, for they are mysteriously decreed by the supreme logic of Providence. That is our case; but once more, the national honor has nothing to do with all this.

The history of a people is more than a succession of facts, it is a series of connected ideas. That precisely is the history we do not have. We have to learn to get along without it, and not to vilify the persons who first noticed our lack. From time to time, in their various searches, our fanatic Slavophils exhume objects of general interest for our museums and our libraries; but I believe it is permissible to doubt that these Slavophils will ever be able to extract something from our historic soil which can fill the void in our souls or condense the vagueness of our spirit. Look at Europe in the Middle Ages: there were no events which were not absolutely necessary in one way or another and which have not left some deep traces in the heart of mankind. And why? Because there, behind each event, you will find an idea, because medieval history is the history of modern thought which tries to incarnate itself in art, in science, in the life of man, and in society. Moreover, how many furrows of the mind have been plowed by this history! . . .

The world has always been divided into two parts, the Orient and the Occident. This is not merely a geographical division, it is another order of things derived from the very nature of the intelligent being— Orient and Occident are two principles which correspond to two dynamic forces of nature; they are two ideas which embrace the whole human organism. . . .

The Orient was first, and it spread waves of light all over the earth from the heart of its solitary meditations; then came the Occident, which, by its immense activity, its quick word, its sharp analysis, took possession of its tasks, finished what the Orient had begun, and finally enveloped it in its vast embrace. But in the Orient, the docile minds, who were prostrated before the authority of time, exhausted themselves in their absolute submission to a venerated principle, and one day, imprisoned in their immovable syntheses, they fell asleep, without any inkling of the new fates in store for them; whereas in the Occident the minds proudly and freely advanced, bowing only to the authority of reason and of God, stopping only before the unknown, with their eyes always fixed on the unlimited future. And you know that they are still advancing, and you also know that since the time of Peter the Great we believe that we are advancing with them.

But here comes another new school. It no longer wants the Occident; it wants to destroy the work of Peter the Great and again follow the desert road. Forgetting what the Occident has done for us, ungrateful towards the great man who civilized us, towards the Europe which taught us, this school repudiates both Europe and the great man; and in its hasty ardor, this newborn patriotism already proclaims that we are the cherished children of the Orient. Why, it asks, do we have to look for lights among the peoples of the Occident? Don't we have in our midst the germs of an infinitely better social order than Europe has? Why don't we leave it to time? Left to ourselves, to our lucid reason, to the fertile principle which is hidden in the depth of our powerful nature, and above all to our saintly religion, we shall soon go beyond those peoples who are a prey to errors and to lies. For what should we envy the Occident? Its religious wars, its Pope, its chivalry, its Inquisition? Truly beautiful things! Is the Occident the native land of science and of all deep things? It is the Orient, as is well known. Let us then withdraw to the Orient, which we touch everywhere and from which erstwhile we derived our beliefs, our laws, and our virtues, all that made us the most powerful people in the world. The old Orient is fading away: well, aren't we its natural heirs? Henceforth it is among us that these wonderful traditions will perpetuate themselves, that all these great and mysterious truths, with whose safekeeping we were entrusted from the very beginning, will realize themselves. Now you understand whence came the storm which beat down upon me the other day, and you see how a real revolution is taking place in our midst and in our national thought. It is a passionate reaction against the Enlightenment and the ideas of the Occident, against that enlightenment and those ideas which made us what we are, and of which even this reaction, this movement which today drives us to act against them, is the result. But this time the impetus does not come from above. On the contrary, it is said that in the upper regions of society the memory of our royal reformer has never been more venerated than it is today. The initiative, then, has been entirely in the hands of the country. Whither will this first result of the emancipated reason of the nation lead us? God only knows! If one truly loves one's country, it is impossible not to be painfully affected by this apostasy on the part of our most highly developed minds towards the things which brought us our glory and our greatness; and I believe that it is the duty of a good citizen to do his best to analyze this strange phenomenon.

We are situated to the east of Europe; that is a positive fact, but it does not mean that we have ever been a part of the East. The history of the Orient has nothing in common with the history of our country. As we have just seen, the history of the Orient contains a fertile idea which, in its time, brought about an immense development of the mind, which accomplished its mission with a stupendous force, but which is no longer fated to produce anything new on the face of the earth. . . .

Believe me, I cherish my country more than any of you. I strive for its glory. I know how to appreciate the eminent qualities of my nation. But it is also true that the patriotic feeling which animates me is not exactly the same as the one whose shouts have upset my quiet existence, shouts which have again launched my boat—which had run aground at the foot of the Cross—on the ocean of human miseries. I have not learned to love my country with my eyes closed, my head bowed, and my mouth shut. I think that one can be useful to one's country only if one sees it clearly; I believe that the age of blind loves has passed, and that nowadays one owes one's country the truth. I love my country in the way that Peter the Great taught me to love it. I confess that I do not feel that smug patriotism, that lazy patriotism, which manages to make everything beautiful, which falls asleep on its illusions, and with which unfortunately many of our good souls are afflicted today. I believe that if we have come after the others, it is so that we can do better than the others; it is so that we may not fall into their faults, their errors, and their superstitions. . . . I believe that we are in a fortunate position, provided that we know how to appreciate it. It is a wonderful privilege to be able to contemplate and judge the world from the height of independent thought, free from unrestrained passions and petty interests which elsewhere disturb man's view and pervert his judgment. More is to come: I am firmly convinced that we are called on to resolve most of the social problems, to perfect most of the ideas which have come up in the old societies, and to decide most of the weighty questions concerning the human race. I have often said it, and I like to repeat it: in a way we are appointed, by the very nature of things, to serve as a real jury for the many suits which are being argued before the great tribunals of the human spirit and of human society.

11
Belinsky: The Miracle of Peter the Great

Vassarion Belinsky (1811–48) was Russia's greatest literary critic and one of the foremost "westerners" among the Russian intelligentsia. In the tradition of Peter Chaadayev, Belinsky spoke out boldly against the encrusted traditionalism imposed on Russian life by church and state, and looked to the European tradition for direction in the reform of Russian society. For Belinsky, therefore, Tsar Peter was one of the great heroes of Russian history.[1]

Russia was cut off from the West at the very beginning of her existence, and Byzantium, as regards civic education, had nothing to offer her other than the custom of blackening the teeth and whiting the face, and gouging the eyes of enemies and malefactors. . . . Then came the Tartar irruption which forged the scattered parts of Russia into unity. This was the great boon of the two centuries of the Tartar yoke; but how great was the mischief it caused Russia, how many were the incidental vices it engrafted? Seclusion of women, slavery in notions and sentiments, the knout, the habit of burying money in the ground and going about in tatters for fear of showing one's self a rich man, corruption in the affairs of justice, Asiatism in ways of life, mental sloth, ignorance, despising of self—in a word, everything that Peter the Great had been eradicating, everything in Russia that was directly opposed to Europeanism. All these ways were not our native characteristics, but engrafted on us by the Tartars. The Russians' very intolerance of foreigners generally was a consequence of the Tartar yoke and not at all of religious fanaticism: the Tartar made everyone who was not a Russian repugnant to the Russian mind—and the word bosurman [infidel] came to be extended from the Tartars to the Germans. Thus the principal faults of our narodnost [nationality] are

[1] V. G. Belinsky, "Russia and the West," in Hans Kohn, ed., *The Mind of Modern Russia* (New York: Harper and Brothers, 1962), pp. 126–28; originally published by Rutgers University Press, 1955, and reprinted with permission of the Rutgers University Press.

acquired and not inherent faults; therefore, we can cast them off, and already we are beginning to do it. . . .

In pre-Petrine Russia there was no trade, no industry, no police, no civil security, no diversity of wants and demands, no military organization, for all was poor and insignificant, since it was not law but custom. And morals? What a sad spectacle! How much there was that was Asiatic, barbaric. How many rites degrading to human dignity there were, e.g., in marriage, and practiced not only by the common people but by the highest personages in the realm! How much there was that was vulgar and coarse in feasting! Compare those heavy repasts, those incredible beverages, those gross kissings, those frequent knockings of the forehead on the floor, those grovelings on the ground, those Chinese ceremonies—compare them with the tournaments of the Middle Ages, the European fêtes of the seventeenth century! . . . Remember what our long-bearded knights and chevaliers were like! Think of our gay ladies lapping up vodka! Men married they knew not whom! Deluded, they beat and tormented their wives in order to raise them by brute force to an angelic status—and if that did not work, they poisoned them with philters. They ate Homerically, drank almost in tubfuls, and kept their wives out of sight, and only when flushed after having eaten several scores of peppery dishes and drunk several buckets of wine and mead would they call them out for a kiss. . . . But, for all that, this has not the slightest bearing on a nation's degradation either morally or philosophically: for it was all the result of our isolation and of Tartar influence. No sooner did Peter open his nation's door to the light of the world than the darkness of ignorance was gradually dispersed—the nation did not degenerate, did not yield its native soil to another people, but became something it had not been before. . . . Yes, gentlemen, defenders of ancient custom, say what you will, but the equestrian statue to Peter the Great on St. Isaac's Square is not enough; altars should be put up to him in all the squares and streets of the great kingdom of Russia! . . .

The point is not whether Peter made us half Europeans and half Russians, consequently neither Europeans nor Russians. The point is are we always to remain in this characterless condition? If not, if we are destined to become European Russians and Russian Europeans, we should not reproach Peter, but rather wonder how he could have accomplished such a gigantic, such an unprecedented task! And so the crux of the matter consists in the words, "shall we"—and we can answer firmly and explicitly that we not only shall become but we are already becoming a people with a character of our own since the reign of Catherine II, and we are making progress therein day by day. We are today the pupils and no longer the zealots of Europeanism; we no longer wish to be either Frenchmen, or Englishmen, or Germans; we want to be Russians in the European spirit. This consciousness is permeating all spheres of our activity and made itself strikingly manifest in our literature with the advent of Pushkin, that great independent and national talent. The fact that the final great act—the utter permeation of our narodnost by Europe—has still not been accomplished and will not be accomplished for a long time merely goes to prove that Peter carried out in thirty years a task that needs centuries. That is why he is a giant among giants, a genius among geniuses, a king among kings. Napoleon himself had a rival in antiquity—Julius Caesar. Our Peter has neither rivals nor models since the beginning of the world; he is akin and equal to no one but himself. . . .

12
Aksakov: Immense Spiritual Evil

Konstantin S. Aksakov (1817–60) represented the "slavophiles," whose admiration of old Muscovite institutions and attitudes was based on a romantic idealization of the national past. Aksakov resented and resisted the changes produced in the years since Peter the Great, and, consequently, blamed Peter for planting the seeds of corruption in Russian life. The following selection is from an essay sent by Aksakov to Tsar Alexander II in order to convince the ruler to roll back the history of Russia to an older and better time.[1]

We must now speak of a period when the government—not the people—violated the principles of Russia's civil order and swerved Russia from her course. The last of the tsars, Theodore, convoked two assemblies during his brief reign: an assembly of the men of service of the state, on matters of precedence which were of interest to the men of service only, and an Assembly of the Land, for the purpose of equalizing taxes and service obligations throughout Russia. While this second assembly was meeting, the Tsar died. It will be remembered that in obedience to the Tsar's will his youngest brother, Peter, was chosen to reign. It is probable that this same Assembly of the Land, which was then meeting in Moscow, confirmed Peter as Tsar, following the wishes of Theodore. However that may be, this Assembly of the Land was dissolved in the name of Peter, then still a minor; but a few years later Peter began to act on his own.

I have no intention of relating in detail the story of Peter's revolution; no intention of disputing the greatness of that greatest of all great men. But the revolution wrought by Peter, despite all its outward brilliance, shows what immense spiritual evil can be done by the greatest genius as soon as he acts alone, draws away from the people, and regards them as an architect does bricks. Under Peter began that evil which is still the evil of our day. Like every evil that is not rem-

[1] K. S. Aksakov, "On the Intellectual State of Russia," trans. Valentine Snow, in Marc Raeff, ed., *Russian Intellectual History: An Anthology* (Harcourt, Brace & World, Inc., 1966), pp. 242–45. Reprinted by permission of the publisher.

edied, it grew worse with the passage of time, and is now a dangerous deep-lying cancer for Russia. I must define this evil.

If the people do not encroach upon the state, the state must not encroach upon the people. Then, and only then, is their union strong and beneficent. In the West there is constant conflict and contention between the state and the people, for they do not understand their proper relationship. Russia knew nothing of such conflict and contention. The people and the government, without mingling, lived in a happy union. Calamities either came from outside or were caused by the imperfections of human nature, and not by a mistaken choice of course or a confusion of concepts. The Russian people remained true to their views and did not encroach on the state; but the state, in the person of Peter, encroached upon the people, invaded their life and customs, and forcibly changed their manners and traditions and even their dress. Attendance at social gatherings was enforced by the police. Even tailors who made clothes in the old Russian style were exiled to Siberia. The men of service who previously, in their private capacity rather than as servants of the state, had identified themselves with the people by sharing their ideas, their way of life, their customs, and their manner of dress, suffered more than anyone from Peter's encroachments upon the moral principles which governed their daily life, and bore the brunt of Peter's revolution. Although the government made the same demands upon all classes of society, including even the peasants, it made them less insistently, and the declared intention not to allow a single peasant to come to the city wearing a beard was later abandoned; instead, beards were taxed. In the end, men of the land were permitted to live and dress as they had done before; but their position in Russia was completely changed. A cleavage had taken place in Russian society. The men of service, or the upper class, had been torn loose from Russian principles, concepts, and customs, as well as from the Russian people; they began to live, dress, and speak like foreigners. The sovereign was displeased with Moscow, and transferred his capital to the edge of Russia, to a new city he had built himself and called by the German name of Sankt-Peterburg. In that city, Peter was surrounded by a whole immigrant population of newly transformed Russians—officials deprived even of their native ground, for the indigenous population of St. Petersburg is foreign.

That is how the breach between the Tsar and the people occurred; that is how the ancient union of the land and the state was torn asunder and replaced by a domination of the state over the land, so that the land of Russia became, as it were, conquered territory and the state its conqueror. That is how the Russian monarch was transformed into a despot, and his willing subjects into slaves held captive in their own country!

The newly transformed Russians, in part driven by force, in part tempted, into adopting foreign ways, soon reconciled themselves to their condition, for the license of their borrowed manners, the ostentation and brilliance of their new society and, lastly, the new rights accorded to the nobles strongly appealed to human passions and weaknesses. Contempt for Russia and for the Russian people soon became an attribute of every educated Russian intent upon aping Western Europe. At the same time the newly transformed Russians, now that their manners and morals were subject to state control and they themselves were in a new position—that of slaves—vis-à-vis the authorities, felt a stirring of political ambition. Among the social classes which had been sundered from the people, particularly among the nobility, a desire for power now manifested itself. Several revolutionary attempts were made and—a thing hitherto unknown—the Russian throne became the illicit plaything of rival factions. Catherine I ascended to the throne unlawfully; unlawful, too, was the ascent of Anne, and on that occasion the aristocracy even planned a constitution, but the attempt fortunately miscarried. Elizabeth came to the throne with the aid of soldiers. Is there any need to speak of the deposition of Peter III? At last, the un-Russian principles imported by Peter the Great found their fruition in the revolt of December 14, a revolt by the upper class, which had been severed from the people, for the soldiers, as we know, were tricked into it.

Such was the conduct of the upper class, which had renounced its Russian principles. And how did the people, who had remained faithful to the Russian principles—the merchants, the townspeople, and particularly the peasants, who more than anyone remained loyal to the Russian ways and spirit—conduct themselves?

During all this time, the people, as should have been expected, remained calm. Is not this calm of theirs the best proof that revolution in any form is contrary to the Russian spirit? The nobles rebelled, but when did the peasants ever rebel against their sovereign? The clean-shaven face and German dress rebelled, but when did the Russian beard and the peasant coat (kaftan) rebel?

The mutiny of the strel'tsy under Peter is a special case; but it was an outbreak of lawlessness rather than a mutiny and, what is more, the strel'tsy found no support among the people. On the contrary, the army recruited from the people zealously fought the strel'tsy and defeated them. In order to win over the bondmen, the strel'tsy tore up the deeds of bondage and scattered them in the streets, but the bondmen declared that they would have none of this freedom, and fought the mutineers. Thus, the people were the first to be outraged by the willful violence of the strel'tsy, and, far from supporting, opposed them. There was, it is true, one terrible uprising in more recent times, but whose name served as its deceptive banner? The name of Peter III, the lawful sovereign. Is not this the final proof that the Russian people —the real mainstay of the throne—are wholly antirevolutionary?

Indeed, so long as the Russian people remain Russian, internal tranquillity and the security of the government are assured. But the system introduced by Peter the Great and the foreign influence which is inseparable from it continue to operate, and we have seen what effect they have had on those many Russians whom they have lured away from the fold. We have seen that the slave mentality—which is generated when the government encroaches upon men's very lives— is accompanied by a spirit of revolt, for a slave is not aware of that dividing line between himself and the government, a line which is perceived by the free man with an independent spiritual life. The slave sees only one difference between himself and the government: he is oppressed, and the government is the oppressor. His base servility can at a moment's notice change to insolent audacity; the slave of today is the rebel of tomorrow, and out of his chains are forged the merciless knives of revolt. The Russian people—that is to say, the common people—adhere to their ancient principles and still resist both the slave mentality and the foreign influence of the upper class. But Peter's system has been in effect for 150 years; it is at last beginning to penetrate to the people, and what reaches the people is its frivolous but harmful aspect. Already in some villages Russian dress is being discarded and even peasants start to talk of fashion, and along with such frivolous matters an alien way of life and alien notions creep in, and Russian principles begin to totter.

As soon as the government takes away the people's inner, communal freedom, it forces them to seek external, political freedom. The longer Peter's system of government continues (although on the face of it, it is not as harsh as it was in his time)—a system so alien to the Russian people, infringing on the freedom of life of the community, restricting the freedom of conscience, thought, and opinion and turning the subject into a slave—the more will foreign ideas infiltrate into Russia, the greater will be the number of people who lose touch with their native Russian soil, the more will the foundations of the Russian land be shaken, and the more terrible will be the revolutionary attempts which in the end will destroy Russia when she has ceased to be Russia. The only danger which threatens Russia is that she may cease to be Russia, and that is where Peter's system of government is leading her. God grant that this may not come to pass!

It will be said that Peter exalted Russia. It is true that he brought her much outward glory, but within her essential integrity he implanted corruption; he sowed the seeds of conflict and destruction in Russian life. Besides, he and his successors were able to perform their glorious exploits by mobilizing the strength of a Russia which had grown and matured in an ancient tradition in another spirit. Our soldiers are still recruited from among the common people, and even the transformed Russians, subjected as they are to a foreign influence, have still not wholly forgotten Russian principles. Thus Peter's state is able to be victorious by drawing on the strength of pre-Petrine Russia; but strength is waning, for Peter's influence is increasingly felt among the people, despite the fact that the government has begun to talk of Russian nationality, even to demand it. But for its good intention to be transformed into a good action, the government must understand the spirit of Russia and embrace Russian principles, which have been rejected since Peter's day. Russia's outward glory, under the emperors, has been truly brilliant, but outward glory is durable only when it stems from inner greatness. The source must not be muddied, nor must it be allowed to dry up. Besides, how can any external brilliance compensate for the loss of inner well-being and inner harmony? What unstable outward glory and unreliable outward strength can compare with stable inner greatness and reliable inner strength? Outward strength can continue to exist only while the inner, albeit undermined, persists in being. If a tree is rotten at the core, it does not matter how strong and thick its bark; one gust of wind and, to the general astonishment, the tree will fall. Russia has stood because her inner strength, which is the heritage of many centuries, has not yet disappeared despite constant abuse and attack, because pre-Petrine Russia still survives in her. Thus the first and highest aim of the people and, naturally, of the government, must be to maintain inner greatness.

13
Klyuchevsky: The Artisan-Tsar

Vasili O. Klyuchevsky (1841–1911), professor at the University of Moscow and mentor of a generation of distinguished Russian historians, is himself acknowledged as the foremost among them. His published lectures, from which the following selection is taken, had an enormous influence. With the passing of the great intellectual struggles of the nineteenth century, Klyuchevsky was able to view Peter more objectively. The emotionally charged atmosphere of praise and blame had faded, and Klyuchevsky struggled to explain the reign of Peter and in the process to examine the ambivalence of his own generation about its relationship to "Europe." He specialized in character sketches, and his presentation of Peter is a classic example which reflects the strengths and contradictions of the artisan-tsar.[1]

In his spiritual composition Peter the Great was one of those simple individuals who need only to be studied to be understood.

In person a giant nearly three *arshini*[2] in stature, he towered a full head above those amongst whom it was his lot to move, and not infrequently found, when performing the ceremony of according the Easter Greeting, that his back ached with the necessity of having to bend forward so frequently. Also his strength was proportionate to his height, for a regular course of the axe and hammer developed the vigour and the dexterity of his muscles until he could twist a silver plate into a scroll with his fingers as easily as he could cleave a flying shred of cloth with a sword. Earlier I have referred to the physical debility which clung to most of the male posterity of the Patriarch Philaret; but whereas Alexis' first wife only perpetuated that debility, Natalia Kirillovna opposed to it a bar—and it was principally after his mother that Peter took. The member of her family whom he most of all resembled was her brother Theodor, as one who had summed up in himself the

[1] V. O. Klyuchevsky, *A History of Russia* (New York: E. P. Dutton and Company, 1926), vol. 4, pp. 25–30, 44–45.
[2] Approximately seven feet.

whole nervous force, and the whole mental agility, of the Narishkin stock, a stock which already had produced many *beaux esprits*, and was later to gain further notoriety in the person of a wit at the Court of Catherine II. A foreign ambassador presented to the two young Tsars in 1683, tells us that Peter was then a lively, handsome lad, and formed a sharp contrast with his brother Ivan, who, seated on the great silver, *ikon*-surmounted throne with Cap of Monomakh pulled down over lowering brows, and eyes looking at no one, almost resembled a lifeless statue, whereas the little Peter, by his side, was sporting jauntily the duplicate Cap manufactured to meet the occasion of the joint Tsarship, glancing cheerfully and trustfully about him, and with difficulty being kept in his seat at all. Later, however, this picture of Peter changes for the worse, when either the shock sustained by his childish intelligence through the horrors of 1682, or an injudicious mode of treating an immature constitution, or (the most likely explanation of all) these two factors combined developed in him a nervous disorder which first showed itself during his twelfth year, and took the form of tremblings of the head, and of the circumstance that, on lapsing into profound thought, or into violent emotion, his features would assume a scowl which wholly marred their comeliness. And since there went with these a birthmark on his right cheek, and a habit of tossing his arms about when walking, he came to be such a remarkable figure that in 1697 the customers in a barber's shop at Saardam easily recognised in the ostensible carpenter from Moscow who was passing the establishment the Tsar of All the Russias—though perhaps they did so the more easily in that there were present in the shop at the time some officious Dutch ex-residents of the Muscovite capital, and that in moments of forgetfulness Peter's large and restless eyes would be wearing a distraught stare, and his mien in general bidding fair to terrify anyone not possessed of the strongest of nerves. As regards portraits of him, we encounter two more frequently than the rest. Of these the first was executed in 1698 by the English artist, Kneller, for William III, and depicts Peter with locks flowing free, and large, rounded eyes, and altogether an animated expression, whilst, despite a certain angularity in the artist's manner of delineation, he has caught something of the vaguely bright, indefinably cheerful expression which is to be noted also in a portrait of Peter's grandmother (a Strieshnev) on his mother's side; whereas the other of the two portraits was executed in 1717 by the Dutch painter Charles Moro, and dates from the period when Peter was returning from Paris (with a view to speedily bringing the Northern War to a conclusion) after an unsuccessful attempt to effect a match between his daughter, the eight-year-old Elizabeth, and the seven-year-old King of France, Louis XV. On this occasion Parisian observers said of him that, even in spite of his fierce and almost barbaric countenance, he fully looked the part of a Sovereign, and proved himself capable of establishing good diplomatico-political relations with anyone whom he deemed likely to prove useful; whilst that he too had had an idea of his own importance is shown by the fact that once, on leaving his Parisian hotel, he flouted all *les convenances* by nonchalantly springing into a carriage which did not belong to him. The truth is that, as always and everywhere he had become accustomed to play the master, he felt himself to be as much master on the Seine as on the Neva. Yet this is not wholly how Moro's artistic vision seems to have regarded him, for in the eyes, as well as in the set of the lips, of the portrait by that artist (which, incidentally, shows a heavier moustache than the portrait by Kneller, a moustache seeming almost to have been secured in place with gum) we can see lurking a sort of half-distressful, half-mournful weariness, so that a beholder might say: "This is the portrait of a man who yearned for a little breathing-space, and, though conscious of his greatness, stood dissatisfied with the accomplishments of his maturity after the self-diffidence of youth." But let it be remembered, that at the time when this portrait was executed Peter was on his way to break his journey at Spa for treatment for the malady which, eight years later, was to bring him to the grave.

In his own home Peter was never anything but a guest, for alike during adolescence and during manhood he was forever either on a journey or engaged in some out-of doors occupation. In fact, if at about the age of fifty he could have halted for a moment, and reviewed his past, he would have seen that his adult years had included few periods when he had not been bound for some destination, when he had not been journeying on one of the tours which took him from Archangel to Azov, and from Astrakhan to Derbent, and from the Neva to the Pruth. And an effect, amongst others, of these years of travelling was to develop, and to fix, in him a restlessness, an itch for changes of scene, a yearning for swift sequences of impressions, which converted haste into a habit, and rendered him a man always in a hurry. In this connection we know even the length of his stride, and can see that, to keep pace with him, the ordinary man must either have run or have progressed by a series of leaps. Besides, he never could remain seated for long: even when taking part in a Court festivity he would leave his chair at intervals, if the function proved protracted, dart into another room, and stretch his legs. And the same restlessness led him, during his earlier years, to cultivate the art of dancing, and to become a familiar and a welcome guest at the merrymakings equally of artisan, of aristocrat, and of tradesman. Nor was his tirelessness in the pursuit of the Terpsichorean art deterred by the fact that he was never able to take any regular course beyond what he picked up at the "eventide practisings of the Lefort establishment." Meanwhile, if not sleeping, travelling, feasting, or inspecting, he was constructing, for his hands were ever at work, and, owing to the fact that he never lost an opportunity of applying them to manual labour, they never lost their horniness. Especially during his younger and more inexperienced days did he never visit a factory or a workshop without engaging in the special process to which it was devoted; in such places he simply could not remain an onlooker, and least of all if he had not previously encountered the operation which he happened at the moment to be investigating. Instinctively his fingers itched for a tool, that he might fall to with the rest. It need hardly be added that this innate taste for the practice of handicrafts developed in him a manual dexterity which, added to his mental alertness, led to his needing merely to scrutinise an unfamiliar task for that task to become his own. In short, a taste originally only a precocious addiction to industrial pursuits and technical labour eventually became a permanent trait. Come what might, he felt that he must learn and master any new accomplishment encountered; and he would do so even before he had considered whether the accomplishment was likely ever to prove useful to him. All this, added to the truly marvellous stock of technical knowledge which he acquired, enabled him, as early in his career as his first foreign tour, to inform the Princes present at the banquet at Koppenburg that he was familiar with the working of fourteen trades. Nor was this an overstatement: never did he need to be present in a factory for long before he had made himself at home with its specialised appliances. One outcome of this was that when death had removed him every place in which he had ever resided was found to be heaped with articles of his own manufacture, such as boots, and chairs, and crockery, and snuffboxes, and the rest, and heaped to a degree which renders it a marvel how he can have gained time for those articles' construction. Also, his mechanical prowess filled him with an immense belief in his own skill, and, amongst other things, he came to consider himself both a first-rate surgeon and a first-rate dentist. Yes, no matter what the horror which his prospective patients might display on realising that they were to be attended by the Tsar in person, he would present himself before them with his instruments, and officiate then and there. And to his dental prowess in particular, and to the magnitude of his dental practice, he left behind him a memorial in the shape of a whole sackful of teeth! But above all other things he loved shipbuilding, and no affair of State could detain him when, instead, there was an opportunity of plying an axe on a wharf. Even in his later years, in the years when he had come to live in his self-built capital of St. Petersburg, he never let a day pass without devoting at least two out of the twenty-four hours to the practice of some nautical pursuit. And, naturally, he attained a proficiency in marine technique which led contemporary opinion to regard him as the best shipwright in Russia, seeing that, besides being able to design and sketch-plan a seagoing craft, he could construct it with his own hands, from keel-laying to the last technical detail. The less wonder, therefore, that he took an immense pride in this manual dexterity, and stinted neither money nor efforts to extend and consolidate the country's shipbuilding industry. True, some may think it curious that a man who had been born in an inland city like Moscow should have come to be a sailor standing in as much need of the breath of the sea as a fish stands of water; but with that it must be remembered that it was to that breath, and to hard physical exercise, that he always attributed the ultimate recovery of his physical constitution, and the annulment of the marriage wrought it through youthful excesses. And to the same cause, probably, was due his invincible, truly sailor-like appetite. At all events, we are told by contemporary writers that a meal never came amiss to him—that, on attending a reception, he could always, no matter whether he had dined or not, sit down again, and fall to with the best. Usually his routine was that he rose at five, and, after lunching from eleven until twelve, retired for a nap (never, even when guests were present, did he omit this item) before rejoining his table-mates for dinner, and with renewed vigour resuming the task of eating and drinking.

Hence there stand before us the factors (1) that early in his career certain untoward incidents of childhood and youth wrenched him clear of the finicking forms of the old Kremlin Court, (2) that the society surrounding him during his later youth was of a nondescript and non-exacting type, (3) that the tenor of his early pursuits early made him handy with the axe, with the lathe, with the saw, and with the correctional cudgel, and (4) that his essentially non-sedentary life converted him into a foe to all ceremony. Indeed, so little could he stomach formality or constraint that, though he was masterful as Tsar, and felt himself at all times and in all places to be overlord, he could not even take part in a State pageant without succumbing to awkwardness and confusion, and, when forced to don ceremonial robes, and stand before the Imperial throne, in order that some newly-accredited foreign ambassador might mouth to him a few high-sounding phrases, would soon be breathing hard, growing red in the face, and dripping with perspiration. Which led him more than ever to strive to be simple and frugal in his own private life; so that it was quite a frequent thing for the monarch whom Europe deemed to be the world's wealthiest and mightiest potentate to be seen stalking the streets of Moscow in slipshod boots, and in stockings which his wife or his daughters had darned. Even his morning receptions of State he would hold in the same rough serge dressing-gown as he had donned when first arising;

and as soon as a reception was over he would exchange the dressing-
gown for the *kaftan* which he hated to discard, and go for a walk or a
drive—in either case, if the season was summer time, and the destination near, bareheaded, and, if driving, with his body thrust into a pair-
horse gig or cabriolet shabby enough once to make a foreign observer
declare that its use would have been scorned by the veriest huckster in
the place. On solemn occasions alone (as when, for example, invited
to attend a wedding) did he resort to his smart *Prokurator-General,*
Yaguzhinski, for the loan of a coach. In other words, he never to the
end abjured the domestic habits of the old-time Russian citizen. In
particular he detested large and lofty rooms, and this was so much the
case that, when travelling abroad, he always avoided the sumptuous
palaces offered for his reception by his hosts. And if it be thought
strange that a man reared on the boundless plains of Central Russia,
a man deeming even the atmosphere of a German valley oppressive,
a man dwelling all his life in the generous, spacious open air, could
not bear to sojourn under a lofty ceiling (as a matter of fact, if he
learnt that he was about to be lodged under a ceiling of the kind, he
always had an under one of canvas constructed for the purpose), there
may lie an explanation of the fact in the modest dimensions of the
little wooden palace at Preobrazhensköe where he had spent his boy-
hood, a palace which a foreign writer of the day declares to have cost
only a hundred thalers to build. However that may be, there can be
no doubt that when he came to build his own palaces around St.
Petersburg he had all of them made small, and their every room,
whether for summer use or for winter, fashioned to a cribbed and
cabined scale. Says the above-quoted foreign observer in conclusion:
"Never can the Tsar stomach a large dwelling." Hence, when Peter
forsook the Kremlin, he forsook with it all the pristine grandeurs of
the Russian Court, and re-ordered things so plainly that in that respect
no establishment of a European crowned head save that of King Friedrich Wilhelm I could vie with his. In fact, he himself would frequently compare the personality of the Prussian Monarch with his
own, and vow that the one cared as little for luxury and extravagance
as the other did. For at Peter's Court there were no chamberlains, no
seneschals, and no expensive plate, and whereas the upkeep of the pre-
Petrine Imperial *ménage* had been accustomed yearly to swallow up
hundreds of thousands of roubles, the new *régime* saw that sum fall to
sixty thousand. . . .

. . . Also, although, during his first foreign tour, he took little note
of the political systems and social observances of the West, he had acu-
men enough to realise that not upon the *knut* and the torture-chamber
had the populousness and the strength of the Western nations grown
up and become based. And to those early lessons learnt from Europe

the first expedition against Azov, and the struggles around Narva and on the Pruth, added a training of a sterner nature, until Peter came really to be aware of his political unpreparedness, and set himself to develop and encourage his consciousness to a habit of political self-education which eventually revealed to him in their entirety the vast blanks in his mental equipment, and turned his mind to such hitherto undreamt-of conceptions as a State, and the people of a State, and justice, and duty, and the functions and obligations of a Sovereign. Yet whilst this augmented Peter's moral sense as Tsar, until self-sacrifice became a permanent rule of his life, it never befell that that augmentation included a rule of suppression of personal addictions, nor did an early riddance of political affectation through early personal misfortunes ever enable Peter's blood wholly to slough the instinct of freewill which from the first had been the dominant element in Muscovite policy, and permit of his mentality grasping the logic of history, and the psychology of his people's life. Yet even for this we can scarcely blame him when we remember that the same factor nearly brought Leibnitz, one of Peter's best counsellors and politicians, face to face with failure, in that for long he held the theory, and caused Peter also to hold it, that culture can be instilled into a country the more that the country stands culturally unprepared! This was why Peter directed his activity as a reformer exclusively to measures needing to be imposed by force, and relied exclusively upon that agency for conferment of popular benefits. Which belief that the impossible was not the impossible, and that the life of a nation could at any time be diverted from its historical channel into an entirely different one, brought it about that Peter's policy, a policy designed to improve the popular labour, only overstrained that labour, and led to reckless and prodigal wastage of human lives and human resources. True, Peter in himself was honourable and sincere; towards his own personality he was as censorious and exacting as he was just and benevolent towards the personalities of others; but the unfortunate point was that the whole bent of his activity insensibly made him a better manipulator of inanimate objects and tools than a manager of living and breathing human beings. He looked upon the latter as so many mechanical instruments, and knew how to use those instruments to the best possible advantage, and had an instinctive sense for the task most suitable for each: yet all the time either inability or disinclination rendered him powerless to put himself in the human instrument's position, or to understand the instrument's nature as that nature really was. The sphere in which these psychological peculiarities found their supremely lamentable expression was the sphere of his own domestic relations. And so much was this the case that even his vast knowledge of his vast dominions never brought him enlightenment as to the one small corner represented by his home and family. Thus to the end of his life he remained a guest on his own hearth. With his first wife he never really lived. His second wife gave him only too much cause to complain. And so far did he fail ever to conciliate the Tsarevitch, his son, that when the time came he could not save that son from baleful influences, and for a while the very existence of his dynasty stood in danger.

To sum up: Peter became, eventually, a ruler wholly different from his predecessors, despite that a certain genetical connection, a certain historical sequence of type and career, is traceable between them all. For first and foremost Peter was a Steward of State, and none of his forerunners had been able to excel him in grasp of, and in discernment of, the prime sources of a nation's wealth. True, the earlier Tsars, of the old dynasty as of the new, also had been Stewards of State; but they had been Stewards of sedentary habit only, soft-handed men, rulers who administered only through the agency of others; whereas Peter issued as a Steward-Labourer-Governor, as a Self-taught State Dispenser, as an Emperor-Artisan.

14

Miliukov: In Advance of His Century

Paul Miliukov (1859–1943) was a distinguished professor of Russian history, an active leader of the Constitutional Democratic Party in the Russian State Duma from 1905 to 1917, and Minister of Foreign Affairs in the Russian Provisional Government of 1917. A leader of the "liberal" or parliamentary forces in Russian society, he viewed Peter from both solid scholarly perspective and strong poiltical persuasion. The following selection is taken from Miliukov's survey of Russian history produced during his exile in Paris after the Russian revolutions.[1]

The reign of Peter the Great marked the beginning of a new era in the history of Russia. The tradition of contemporary Russia, of civilized Russia, dates from this period. The chief characteristics of this new historical epoch, the groundwork for which was laid before Peter became tsar, were that Russia unmistakably assumed the position of a European power and became an important factor in international relations, while at home a new class came into being and immediately took on the character of a privileged nobility. The advent of Peter the Great was the inception of the gradual shaping of generations that, after long and rather close subjection to foreign influences, were to gain more and more freedom and finally to create Russian civilization by assimilating the genius of the people.

Historians have long disputed the personal part played by Peter the Great in this evolution of the Russian spirit. For his partisans, his role is very important; his opponents, on the other hand, refuse to recognize any merit in him and argue that his only accomplishment was to force Russia into an abnormal course. By way of differing lines of ar-

[1] From Paul Miliukov, Charles Seignobos, and L. Eisenmann, *A History of Russia,* translated by Charles Lam Markmann (New York: Funk & Wagnalls, 1968), vol. 1, pp. 212–13, 232–33, 238, 304–5, 309–10, 330–31. French Edition by Librarie Ernest Leroux, 1932. Translation copyright © 1968 by Funk & Wagnalls. All rights reserved. Reprinted by permission of Funk & Wagnalls.

gument, both sides arrived at the same conclusion: the major factor in Peter's work of reform was his will or his whim.

Recent historical studies have shown that there are closer ties than was generally believed between the epoch of Peter the Great and its immediate predecessor; the result of these studies is to deny the existence of an interruption of continuity that some scholars ascribe to this period in Russian history, and instead to view the reigns of Peter and his predecessors as successive stages of a single organic historical evolution. If, as a result of that evolution, the Russian nation acquired a more European character, this shows that all the bases of Russia's development place her in Europe rather than in Asia, even though she was, so to speak, an intermediary between these two parts of the world. But, even while they establish the organic character of Russia's historical evolution, these studies, in contrast to those that preceded them, seek to diminish the personal part played by the reforming tsar.

What exactly was Peter's personal part? In a general way it can be said that Peter's period marked Russia's transition from an unconscious, even spontaneous, evolution, the fruit of her national genius, to a more conscious evolution, more directed toward a goal, more deliberate. Nevertheless Peter's first reforms, so dissimilar to the general character of his work, seemed rather the product of a caprice, and broke into the general evolution. It is in this sense that Peter the Great can be called "the first Russian revolutionary." Indeed his first efforts at reform were rather destructive in nature; it was only later that he embarked on a labor of reconstruction. This transition from the unconscious and the impulsive to the conscious and the systematic was the distinguishing characteristic of the great reform that Peter launched and that marked a transition period. . . .

All the innovations of 1699–1700 applied to the externals of life. We shall observe infinitely more important alterations that imposed vast sacrifices on the population, that radically modified the structure of the state itself, and that are nevertheless virtually forgotten today. For, when we speak of Peter's work, which divided the history of Russia into two sections, our imagination turns first of all toward the outward transformation of the population, precisely because that was what made the strongest impression on his contemporaries, for it symbolized the destruction of the old customs hallowed by religion and consequently it meant the upheaval of beliefs themselves. If we consider the reforms of the same character undertaken today in less developed countries, we shall be able to understand the importance that the people attached to traditional symbols; it is not so long since the removal of the Turk's fez and his wife's veil shocked the most profound beliefs and threatened to bring on a popular rebellion. The later this trend toward secularization appears in a nation's life, the more difficult the change appears and the more it threatens to arouse the resentment of the mass of the people, especially since, as a rule, it occurs under foreign influences. In Russia this change was particularly grievous, and it was just in those years 1699–1700 that popular indignation against Peter exploded with the greatest force. . . .

The archives of the Preobrazhensky *prikaz,* which terrorized all Russia under its terrible chief, Romodanovsky—"a man who resembled a monster," as Prince Kurakin expressed it—are full of instances of popular indignation and of the reasons for it. "The tsar cuts off beards and fraternizes with Germans; our religion too has become German," one man said. According to another, "the tsar lives according to foreign styles, and eats meat on Wednesday and Friday; he did not observe the fast of St. Philip. He ordered everyone to wear German clothes. He eliminated the patriarchate so that he could rule alone and not have any rivals. On 1 January 1700 he ordered the celebration of the new year and thus he broke the covenant of the Holy Fathers. The years of God have been destroyed and the years of Satan proclaimed." Peter was "destroying the Christian faith, ordering men to shave their beards, wear German clothes, and smoke tobacco. I have come to Moscow to confound him," *Posadsky* Andrey Ivanov announced when he went to the capital from Nizhni-Novgorod expressly in order to make the tsar listen to reason.

These few instances show that in the eyes of the people the renunciation of the old ways was tantamount to a betrayal of the faith. While the division between the ruling class and the people that was caused by Nikon's "new faith" had occurred well before the time of Peter the Great, it was nevertheless not yet total and seemed unlikely to become final. The two opposing camps clashed in the same theater and employed the same weapons. Those who were beaten one day in a religious dispute cherished the hope of having their revenge later that same day, or perhaps the next. The masses, who took no direct part in the clergy's quarrel, could quietly wait for the day when the solution to the conflict would have been found by the "readers" of the holy books, the "intellectuals" of the era. This state of mind was still persisting at the time of the revolts of the *stryeltsi* in 1682 and 1689. The rebels, who were exhorted to defend the "ancient faith," could reply: "That is the business of the patriarch; as far as we are concerned, we are satisfied to examine the truth in order to know why the old books have been repudiated and what the heresies were that they contained." But no further hesitancy could survive after Peter's first reforms. The position taken by the tsar, whether interpreted from the old or the new point of view, was "outside the faith." The forces of the opposition mounted because they were defending the cause of religion against secularization, and the keynote of this opposition was understandable to all and hence very popular, for it denounced what all could see: the new clothes, the shaven faces, tobacco. By fighting the Greeks, who had deformed the ancient texts, those texts through which the Muscovite thaumaturges had saved their souls, Nikon's enemies had already evidenced a certain nationalist spirit. Now, turning against a social class wrapped up in foreign garments, popular opposition became essentially nationalist; as we have seen, the foreigners' quarter of Moscow was threatened with a veritable St. Bartholomew's Day. . . .

Such was the social climate in which Peter's reform evolved. For the first time the ideology of the masses was discrete from that of the "Europeanized" ruling class; socially, it was "German" dress that showed the demarcation between them. While the people remained hostile to reform, it was the ruling class that held political and social power from the eighteenth century on. It was indeed this class that, thanks to Peter, gave rise to the first group of men of European culture, who were later to be called the *Intellizhentsya,* the Russian intellectuals. . . .

Radical and despotic, Peter's reform allowed nothing to stop it; it equalized all individuals and in this sense it was democratic. Nonetheless, as a result of the upheavals that it entailed, Russian society was little by little to assume an aristocratic character: first of all, the old class of "men of service," which the inception of regular military service had modernized and rejuvenated by infusing it with outside elements, became a closed class; this in its turn became the nucleus of the future nobility, called on to govern the state without regard for the positions held by its members in the service of the tsar. While this last development merely began under Peter and was completed only under his successors, the signs that foreshadowed it were rather significant in the final years of his reign.

Peter's first measures, however, gave hardly any indication of what was to follow. Had he not sent the grooms from his stables to his *potyeshny* regiments in order, as Kurakin said, "to humiliate the great families"? Had he not also, with a view to his military projects, very publicly proclaimed that the Russian military class should "serve" the state? The evasion of military service was only too widespread a habit in those days. Pososhkov reported a saying that was common among the landowners: "God grant that we can serve the great sovereign without ever taking a sword from its scabbard!" During the campaigns, these warriors "went into hiding in the woods and gullies by whole squads, with no desire but to return to their homes." Peter "snatched them by force" from their refuges under the threat of cruel punishments. Local supervision of military service by landowners having been abolished at the same time as territorial recruiting, he replaced it with extensive surveys of the nobility and made a meticulous census of adolescents and young men. In 1704 (one of the most difficult years, as we have seen), he made an inspection of more than eight thousand young men recruited in all the provinces: five or six hundred "of the noblest," including princes (Golitsyns and Cherkasskys, among others), were distributed among the guard regiments as ordinary soldiers. In 1712 the young men of Moscow were sent in a mass to Petersburg to be passed in review. In 1714 every nobleman between the ages of twenty and thirty was called upon to register with the Senate under the penalty of the confiscation of his fortune. By virtue of a ukase of 1722, any nobleman who did not appear for the inspection incurred the risk of being "stigmatized," of undergoing "civil death"; thus outlawed, he could be killed or despoiled by anyone who chose to do so. But the fact that it was continually necessary to renew and increase these penalties is sufficient evidence of their ineffectiveness. The nobility continued to evade service, but the methods changed: instead of going to ground in their own estates, the nobles clung to the rearguard, and, when battles were to be fought, if Pososhkov is to be believed, they arranged for some sinecure, or, better still, some profitable assignment; or else, to quote Pososhkov still, they followed the example of that Zolotarev who arranged to be replaced by an impoverished nobleman to whom he gave his name, his horse, and his orderly, "while he coursed over the countryside with a team of six horses and ruined his neighbors."

In spite of such defections the principle of compulsory public service had been established, and the constant wars, which turned soldiers of fortune into a regular army, made this service everlasting. . . .

It was never Peter's intention to institute serfdom. When finally he took full account of the consequences of his legislation, he was the first to be appalled. He strove in vain to diminish at least the visible evidences of the evolution toward serfdom that were well under way: in 1721 he instructed the Senate "to put an end to the retail sale of persons, which does not exist in any country and gives rise to cries of distress. In the event that it should be impossible to abolish it entirely, let sales at least be made of entire families as units, not of individual serfs." It was in vain that the peasant Pososhkov—far in advance of his day—endeavored to obtain a law establishing rents and obligations and separating the peasant's land from that of his owner; it was in vain that he evolved his guiding conception that "landowners are not the eternal masters of peasants." The subjugation of the peasant, which was to continue for one and a half centuries in a hitherto unknown form, had begun. When the state ceased its intervention in the relations between landowners and peasants, when it made the landowners responsible for the peasants, it abandoned them to the mercy of their masters. It was thus that serfdom was inaugurated in fact, with all its legal vices and all its moral repulsiveness. . . .

It must be admitted that these criticisms by Peter's contemporaries are considerably more convincing than anything that later defenders of the ancient Russian traditions were able to say against the reforms. Most of these criticisms are reasonable and well founded. The picture of the domestic economy of the Russian landowner, for instance, is quite accurate: that economy did not easily lend itself to the ruinous scale of living in the capital or in a military camp, which compelled the landowner to be absent from his estates for many years and sowed chaos in his affairs. Similarly, it is easy to ascertain what was artificial and unnecessary in the capricious, incoherent, and often unreasoned activity that Peter devoted to his foreign policy and his military projects. When twentieth-century Russia had lost all Peter's conquests on the Baltic except Petersburg and the capital had been moved back to Moscow, this artificial side emerged more sharply than before. Peter's relations with the little German courts were much closer than Russia's interests required them to be. He offered Russian soldiers to anyone who asked. Under his direct successors, the effects of these unnecessary interventions were much more acutely felt, and it was only under Catherine II that a true Russian national policy appeared. In the same way, too, the advantages of Moscow's central position and the inconveniences and perils arising out of Petersburg's situation too close to the border thrust themselves into prominence. The creation of that new capital in the Finnish marshes and in the midst of peoples of other races might have seemed the whim of a despot who had made up his mind to violate the laws of history and nature.

All the criticisms that we have listed can be summed up in one: Peter's reform, which from many points of view was ahead of his time, was premature and beyond the capacities of a country as poor and as backward as Russia. Nevertheless, over the next two centuries, events justified what was essential in it. Peter had foreseen the road that Russia was destined to follow. His activity could not be understood by his contemporaries because it foreshadowed a distant future in which an active foreign policy, a lively foreign commerce, and a national fleet would be essential requirements for Russian national independence. His contemporaries, whose views we have reported, saw only their immediate needs—that is, the goals that the Russia of their time was capable of setting for herself and achieving; that is why their criticisms contain a substantial element of truth and why on the part of a man like Prince D. M. Golitsyn opposition was as natural as it was inevitable. The effects of these criticisms we have already seen: the simplification of the overly complicated and excessively costly administrative system that Peter had instituted. We shall observe others. But this reaction was only temporary, and it could not prevent Russia from following the historic furrow that Peter had so deeply and strongly plowed in the virgin soil of his country.

15
Pokrovsky: The Bankruptcy of Peter's System

Michael N. Pokrovsky (1868–1932) was one of the first great Marxist historians of Russia. The following selection is from a five-volume work he produced between 1910 and 1912. This study suffered the tribulations of a pioneering Marxist work and was the subject of numerous attacks and revisions in the Soviet period. It was Pokrovsky's task to find a place for Peter's work in the unfolding dialectic of history.[1]

So long as Russia was under the control of the nobility, the work of administration had been directly performed by those who held the political power; in the seventeenth century the vassals of the Muscovite sovereign, the military landholders, had collected taxes, had administered justice, and had maintained a police system just as they had done a century earlier, and as, in reality, they were to do two centuries later if we consider the social meaning of the phenomenon rather than its juridical formulation. The uniform background presented by the regime of the nobility, however, is very distinctly marred at the end of the seventeenth and beginning of the eighteenth centuries; for the shifting of the economic centre of gravity could not fail to affect the apportionment of power among the several groups of society. The springtide of commercial capitalism brought with it something absolutely unprecedented for Muscovite Russia, a bourgeois administration.

Russian historians have long since described how on the border line between the two centuries, in 1699, the nobles' voevoda, a man who, in return for service and wounds, had been appointed to his post to "feed himself to satiety," had to surrender his post to the townsman's burmister, a man who was something between "the responsible financial agent of the government" and (but more like this latter) an

[1] M. N. Pokrovsky, *History of Russia from the Earliest Times to the Rise of Commercial Capitalism*, ed. Jesse D. Clarkson (Bloomington, Indiana: University Prints and Reprints, 1966), pp. 289–90, 326–27. Reprinted by permission of Academic International, formerly University Prints and Reprints, Hattiesburg, Mississippi.

accountable steward. But with their customary faith in the miraculous power of the state, these historians have not been arrested by the fact; for why should not the state hand over local administration to the merchants if it suited its convenience? Had not even Ivan the Terrible boasted that from stones he could raise up the seed of Abraham? To make a trader a judge and administrator was many times easier than this. Yet if we remember what a gigantic smash had accompanied the transfer of the administration from the hands of the boyars, i.e., the representatives of large landholding, into the hands of the nobles, i.e., the representatives of middling landholding, we shall be able to understand how great a leap was the transfer of authority, even though only of local authority, into the hands of men who did not belong to the landholding class at all.

There is, perhaps, no better illustration of the revolutionary, catastrophic character of Peter's reforms than this change, which it has become customary to explain by meagre considerations of state convenience. To deprive one class of power and transfer it to another simply in order "more reliably to regulate financial responsibility" (as Mr. Milyukov explains the reform of 1699)—this is something that not one state in the world has done, simply because not one could do it.

It is true, Petrine Russia did not succeed in making the transfer for long; in less than thirty years the nobles' state had regained the upper hand. But even the attempt could not have been made had there not existed a very special correlation of forces; it needed that alliance of the bourgeoisie with the foremost members of the landholding class to which we have already referred. When the new feudal aristocracy had no further use for its bourgeois ally, the latter had to return to its former political insignificance. But it immediately became clear that without this meagre support the "supreme lords" themselves were quite unable to hold their ground; coming face to face with the nobility, which had been pushed into the background, they rapidly had to give way to it, and the nobles again steadied themselves in the saddle, this time for almost two centuries. . . .

Bourgeois on the surface, Petrine society continued to be military at the core. The mention of "soldiers" may have inspired in the reader the illusion that we were speaking of something new, of a sort of military democracy. Nothing of the sort; the kernel of Peter's Guard was composed of "princes and simple nobles." This vital fact had at once impressed itself on foreign observers, who strove to explain it according to their lights. "He is gracious with all," says the French diplomat Campredon, "and pre-eminently with the soldiers, most of whom are children of princes and lords, who are serving him as a pledge of their fathers' loyalty." In fact, even under Peter, the nobility had begun to elaborate the central organ which was to aid it in resuming authority under his successors. The thin bourgeois veil had no more changed the nature of the Muscovite state than had the German cloak changed the nature of the Muscovite man. When Peter died, only the small group of "supreme lords," devoid of social support among the masses, stood between the nobility and power. The "supreme lords," having failed to create a bourgeoisie, were like a staff without an army, while the old military-serving class, clad in the Preobrazhensky uniform, merely awaited a convenient moment to "break the lords' heads for them."

The military force very quickly managed to make itself a political force. Scarcely had Peter closed his eyes in death when the Guard was master of the situation. Without the consent of the Guardsmen no one could ascend the Russian throne, so lately filled by "their colonel."

The impact of commercial capitalism on Russia had cost her very dear; nor were Russia's losses to be measured by her expenditures in men and money. No "active policy" can ever dispense with such outlays, and in this particular Russia in 1725 did not differ essentially from France at the moment of the death of Louis XIV, from Prussia at the close of the Seven Years' War, or even from England at the end of her struggle with Napoleon. The population had been ruined and had scattered. The effects were felt long before the close of the war; by 1710 the loss of population, as compared with the last pre-Petrine census, has been calculated by Mr. Milyukov as reaching 40 per cent in some places. However unreliable the statistics of the time (even contemporaries had no confidence in the census of 1710), they give a fairly definite general impression, especially where they are supplemented by comments. Of the province of Archangel the official document remarks that "losses of homesteads and their inmates have appeared because the men have been taken as recruits, as soldiers, as carpenters, to St. Petersburg as workers, as settlers, as smiths." Of the 5,356 homesteads "lost" in the Shekhona country, 1,551 had been abandoned because of conscription for the army or for labour on public works, and 1,366 because of flights. To foreigners it seemed that the central provinces had been absolutely depopulated thanks to the Northern War; and though this opinion must be taken with the same reserve as the assertion of these same foreigners that the clay-soil near Moscow was among "the best lands in Europe," this summary impression was not pure fantasy. A document of 1726, which bears the signatures of almost all the "supreme lords," accepts unquestioningly the following "reasons" for non-payment of the soul tax: "since the census many peasants who were able to earn money by their labour, have died and been taken as recruits and run away . . . while of those who now by labour can get money to meet the state taxes there remain but a small number." Nor did the "supreme lords" dispute a reference to the decline of peasant economy: "besides that, for several years now there have been crop failures, and in many places the peasants sow little grain, and those who sow are compelled to sell the grain in the ground to meet state taxes, and hence they go running into far places where it would be impossible to seek them out." Yet in this second quotation we already have an explanation of peasant ruin by other than political factors; for obvious reasons the official document is silent about the social causes, which were, however, clearly evident to foreigners, who, in accounting for the depopulation of central Russia assigned to the "savage dealings of the masters" as much weight as to the Northern War.

The bankruptcy of Peter's system lay not in the fact that "at the price of the ruin of the country Russia was raised to the rank of a European power" but in the fact that, regardless of the ruin of the country, this goal was not attained. Foreigners in Russian service rated the might of Peter's empire far lower than did foreigners looking on from a distance, or than later historians have done. Field-Marshal Münnich, in an intimate conversation with the Prussian envoy, Mardefeld, did not conceal from him that the Russian troops were in a very lamentable condition: the officers were good for nothing; among the soldiers were many untrained recruits; there were no cavalry horses at all—in a word, had there appeared another opponent like Charles XII, he might with 25,000 men have settled accounts with the whole "Muscovite" army. And he said this only two years after the Peace of Nystadt, so brilliantly celebrated! The fleet was no better off; only the galleys were worth anything, and while they were very practical for a little war in the fiords of Finland, they were not fit for the open sea. For the sake of speed, ships were built of green wood; they rotted with extraordinary rapidity in the fresh waters of the Kronstadt haven. This was one of the chief reasons for Peter's attempt to transfer his fleet base to Rogervik (later "Baltic Port," near Reval), situated close to the open sea, where the water was salt. But Peter's engineers could not cope with the large waves; every violent storm swept away all the fruits of their toil, so that the construction of Rogervik became synonymous with the labours of Sisyphus. The personnel of the fleet was no better than its materiel. Peter was soon disappointed in his foreign-trained "midshipmen" and by the end of his reign was no longer sending them abroad to study. The condition of the sailors is best indicated by a report one foreign diplomat made to his government, a report made at the very time of the magnificent masquerades in celebration of victory over the Swedes. "By way of anticipating disorders and preserving tranquillity the number of the guard in the residency here was doubled. I was told that the cause of the multiplicity of precautions taken on this occasion lay in the fact that a very considerable number of sailors, whose wages, despite the order given by the tsar before his departure that they should be paid off, had not been paid, and who had not a piece of bread, had conspired to gather in a crowd and loot the houses of the inhabitants of the residency here."

16
Soviet Academy of Sciences: Absolutism and the Police-Bureaucratic State

Recent Soviet evaluations of Peter have emphasized the strengthening of the absolute monarchy and the emergence of the police-bureaucratic state. The work from which the following selection is taken was produced by scholars of the Academy of Sciences of the USSR, and the specific selection was written by A. I. Pashkov, Corresponding Member of the Academy.[1]

The Russian state of this period was feudal-absolutist, that is, it represented a definite stage in the development of the feudal, nobility state. Peter I strengthened the absolute monarchy and brought about the victory of absolutism in Russia. The feudal state was "the organ of the nobility for suppression of the enserfed peasants. . . ." In the absolute monarchy the real power remained in the hands of the feudalists.

The class nature of the Russian state of this period and the character of the Petrine reforms are clearly defined by I. V. Stalin: "Peter the Great did much for the elevation of the class of pomeshchiki and the development of the rising merchant class. He contributed much to the creation and strengthening of the national state of the pomeshchiki and merchants."

The far-reaching and complex task of Russia—to eliminate the backwardness of the country—was closely connected with the immediate task to gain military victory in the struggle for sea outlets. Both of these aims forced Peter to deal resolutely with the economic problems of the country. He formulated a broad program of economic

[1] A. I. Pashkov, ed., *A History of Russian Economic Thought: Ninth Through Eighteenth Centuries,* ed. John Letiche, translated with the collaboration of Basil Dmytryshyn and Richard A. Pierce (Berkeley: University of California Press, 1964), pp. 245–49. Reprinted by permission of The Regents of the University of California.

transformation which included: 1) the establishment of heavy industry and the development of handicrafts; 2) the improvement of external and internal trade; 3) the promotion of agriculture; 4) the extension of the water routes of communication; 5) the advancement of the finances of the country.

The economic functions of the Russian feudal state were narrow and one-sided. The problem of developing the productive forces of the country remained outside the interests of [central] government authority. Only in the second half of the seventeenth century did the [central] government begin to concern itself with economic tasks other than those of requisition and taxation and to adopt measures for the development of trade and industry. Ordyn-Nashchokin emphasized the development of the national economy as the immediate task of the state. The economic reforms of the first quarter of the eighteenth century marked the further progress of political thought and government activity in this direction.

Peter I's understanding of the economic tasks and functions of the state was closely connected with the very nature of absolutism and the police-bureaucratic state. The latter is characterized by the fact that the state power, based on officialdom, the police, and the army, entirely suppresses the personal rights of the lower classes of society, establishes unlimited interference in the life of the subjects, and introduces powerful regulations as well as complex enforced guardianship. This enforcement, guardianship, and supervision of the feudal noble state also embrace the realm of economic life. As chief of a feudal-absolutist, police-bureaucratic state, Peter I utilized state power as a weapon to suppress the resistance of the toilers against their exploiters, as a weapon of supra-economic compulsion. He significantly extended the application of forced serf labor in the country, and chained the peasant to the landowner more relentlessly than before.

Under Peter, treasury needs continued to play a central, but no longer exclusive, role in the economic policies of the state. Although always concerned about revenue (indeed, his fiscal policy was unprecedented in its energy and scope) Peter devoted serious attention to the development of the productive forces of the country, the growth of technology, and the increase of the productivity of labor. This was the first time that Russia witnessed extensive state activity in these fields.

The political ideology of Peter received literary expression in a prominent treatise of the time, The Right of Monarchian Will by Feofan Prokopovich. The cornerstone of this philosophy was that state power has not only rights over its subjects, but also obligations to them. These obligations center in the responsibility of the state for the "general welfare," the "public good." Consequently, Peter laid a broad legislative foundation for measures of state authority. "We hereby declare that we always have a diligent interest in the spread of general well-being and benefits to our subject merchants and to all other arts and crafts which all other wealthy states have and foster," notes the Tsar's 1718 charter to Savelov, a member of a provincial court, and to the Tomilin merchants for the establishment of a mill. The "Regulation of the Manufacturing College" also refers to the increase in Russian manufactories "for the general welfare and prosperity of the subjects. . . ." In his historic speech on the conclusion of peace with Sweden (October 22, 1721), Peter I said, "One must work for the general well-being."

The principle of "general welfare" is customary in the theories of absolutism and is found among all spokesmen of the absolutist variant of the theories of "national law" both in Russia and in Western Europe. Under the pretext of the "general Welfare" of the subjects, absolutists and their theoreticians everywhere defended autocratic power. In Russia the contemporary of Peter I, Feofan Prokopovich, used this same idea as the basis for absolutism.

The theoreticians of absolutism and the absolutists present the principle of "general welfare" as a supra-class principle, and the state power is portrayed as an extra-class force equally concerned with the entire population. In actuality the feudal state is the political organization of the class of feudalists. In a society where some classes are exploited by others, the state defends not only the general national interests of the given country against other countries, but above all, and mainly, the interests of the ruling class against the oppressed classes of the country. The subjugation of the exploited and the suppression of their resistance represent significant functions of the feudal-absolutist state. Expanding these ideas of "general welfare" and "public good" as the basic task of unlimited monarchy, the theoreticians of absolutism and the absolutists themselves mask the two-faced class nature of the feudal state. In feudal society the "general welfare" is above all the welfare of the noble class and the merchants. Security from external foes, the growth of culture in the country, and the development of productive forces are accomplished at the expense of the toiling, oppressed masses; and the benefits of culture and of the development of technology and productive forces are utilized first of all by the ruling classes—the nobility and merchants.

At a specific historical level in the evolution of society, absolutism was a political form corresponding to the progressive tendencies of the development of society, expressing itself in a struggle for the creation and establishment of a national state as opposed to feudal disunity.

Peter I attached great significance to the activity of the state in economic life. In his view the state was a force directing the economic development of the country, and state legislation was the mighty lever of this development. The issuing of corresponding law decrees, regulations, and instructions concerning economic life and the struggle for their implementation were, therefore, one of the most important aspects of Peter's state activity. He maintained that the state is an organ immediately responsible for broad economic activity. Peter energetically developed the economic activity of the state and realized, to a high degree for that time, the construction of crown industrial enterprises, canals, sheep farms, stud farms, and the development of state, domestic and foreign trade.

But the economic functions of the state were interpreted by Peter I in a much broader form than the direct economic activity of the organs of the state. The state, in Peter's view, ought in all ways to call forth and encourage private initiative and private enterprise so as to teach its subjects the rules of rational husbandry and sensible economy and to show people how to be "good economists." The state should implant new forms of organization for labor and new techniques. The means of implanting the rules of good economy by the state are understood in broad terms. Here are both direct compulsion and propaganda: practical initiative of the state, aid to the people, encouragement of private enterprise, and its compulsion. Peter broadly applied these various methods of implanting new forms of economy, and they were often combined.

He considered it necessary to use propaganda widely to urge the wisdom of the economic measures being introduced by the state. The decrees not only informed the subjects of the norms obligatory for execution, but they were also utilized as a means of propaganda in favor of the measures taken. Thus, for example, the decree directing that Russian leather be made only with train oil, and not with pitch, explained the reason for the measure: leather made with pitch admits moisture and soon wears out. In a decree directing the use of the scythe and rake in harvesting grain instead of the sickle, there is the explanation that other countries work primarily with the scythe and rake. Peter attached great significance to the wide distribution of decrees and other laws among the people, and he required these to be printed and disseminated and the most important to be displayed in the churches, fairs and trading places ("to be spread by the town crier").

Guardianship, regulation, and compulsion in the implementation of new forms of economic activity are looked upon as unavoidable because of the backwardness and ignorance of the people in questions of economic life and their distrust of new ways. In one of the outstanding laws—the decree of November 5, 1723—concerning the spread of factories in Russia, admitting that few volunteers are willing to start factories, Peter writes: "because our people are like children about their learning, they will not learn the alphabet until they are forced by their master; at first they complain, but when they learn, then they are thankful, as is evident from contemporary affairs; not everything has been accomplished willingly which has brought fruits, and about many things one hears praise; in manufactories we apply not only proposals, but we also force and instruct and use machines and other measures to teach you how to be a good economist."

In the same spirit a decree establishing a company for trade with Spain was issued: "because everyone knows that our people will not undertake anything without compulsion: as a result the Commerce College shall have direction like a mother over her children until they are mature and administer this new affair."

In accordance with this broad understanding of the economic tasks and functions of the state, the state apparatus was also reorganized. Characteristically, of the number of state colleges created under Peter (in place of the outmoded system of departments) almost half were economic colleges: the Mining College, managing the mining industry; the Manufacturing College, taking charge of all other industries; the Commerce College, supervising foreign commerce and trade in ship building; the Finance College, handling the collection of state revenues; the State Control College, dealing with state expenditures. The Chief Magistrate supervised internal trade and handicrafts. For the management of agriculture there was no special college, but the development of agriculture was included in the functions of the Finance College.

Bibliographical Note

Biographies of Peter the Great which are available in English include the classic by Voltaire, *History of the Russian Empire in the Reign of Peter the Great*. The best of the nineteenth-century works include a two-volume study by Eugene Schuyler, *Peter the Great* (1890), and a work translated from the French, Kasimir Waliszewski, *Peter the Great* (1897). More recent works include those of Stephen Graham (New York, 1929), Constantin de Grunwald (New York, 1956) and Ian Grey (New York, 1960). The treatment of Peter by the eminent Russian historian Vasili Klyuchevsky is now available in an excellent translation by Liliana Archibald (New York, 1963). Fine shorter works on Peter include B. H. Sumner, *Peter the Great and the Emergence of Russia* (New York, 1951). The reader might also be interested in L. Jay Oliva, *Russia in the Era of Peter the Great* (Englewood Cliffs, 1969). Contemporary and historical opinions of Peter have been gathered in Marc Raeff, ed., *Peter the Great: Reformer or Revolutionary?* (Boston, 1963). Specialized studies are available in B. H. Sumner, *Peter the Great and the Ottoman Empire* (Oxford, 1949), and C. B. O'Brien, *Russia Under Two Tsars, 1682–1689* (Berkeley, 1952).

Foreign language treatments include the best recent work on Peter, R. Wittram, *Peter I, Czar und Kaiser* (Gottingen, 1964), and the still-provocative work of P. Miliukov, C. Seignobos, and L. Eisenmann, *Histoire de Russie*, 3 volumes (Paris, 1932). In Russian the reader might survey N. Ustryalov, *Istoriya tsarstvovaniya Petra Velikago*, 6 volumes (Saint Petersburg, 1858–63), and Sergei Soloviev, *Istoriya Rossii s drevneishikh vremen* (Saint Petersburg, n.d.), vol. 18. Peter's papers began to be published before the Russian revolutions and the task was taken up again after World War II, (*Pisma i bumagi imperatora Petra Velikago*). Soviet views of the Petrine era are examined in Cyril E. Black, ed., *Rewriting Russian History* (New York, 1956). A collection of contemporary accounts of Peter's reign will be found in Peter Putnam, ed., *Seven Britons in Imperial Russia* (Princeton, 1952), and in Baron Korb, *Scenes from the Court of Peter the Great* (New York, 1921). Petrine literature is surveyed in Harold Siegel, ed., *The Literature of Eighteenth-Century Russia*, 2 volumes (New York, 1967). There is a fine Soviet historical novel on Peter by Alexei Tolstoi, *Peter the First* (New York, 1961).

Index

GREAT LIVES OBSERVED

Gerald Emanuel Stearn, *General Editor*